The Coats Book of
LACECRAFTS

The Coats Book of
LACECRAFTS

JEAN KINMOND

B T Batsford   *London*

© Jean Kinmond 1978
First published 1978
ISBN 0 7134 0783 2

Filmset by
Servis Filmsetting Ltd, Manchester
Printed in Great Britain by
Butler & Tanner Ltd, Frome
for the publishers
B T Batsford Ltd
4 Fitzhardinge Street
London W1H 0AH

Contents

GENERAL INFORMATION

Mercer-Crochet Cotton

Coats Mercer-Crochet Cotton is the ideal thread for crochet, tatting and knitting. It is easy to work with, soft, glossy and of uniform thickness; washes beautifully, never loses its colour or becomes 'stringy', and preserves the beauty of the design – qualities which are of the utmost importance to the craft.

Coats Mercer-Crochet Cotton is available in a variety of sizes. Ticket No.20 is the most popular and has the largest shade range. Ticket No.10 is thicker and has a much smaller shade range. Ticket No.40 is finer than No.20 and has a good shade range. Ticket No.60 is finer than No.40 and has a small shade range.

The size or texture of a design may be altered by changing the size of Mercer-Crochet Cotton.

Coats Mercer-Crochet Cotton 50 g balls
This thread is now available in a limited shade range in ticket No.20. The shades are as follows: White, 402 (Lt Rose Pink), 442 (Mid Buttercup), 469 (Geranium), 503 (Coral Pink), 508 (Lt Marine Blue), 573 (Laurel Green), 582 (Straw Yellow), 608 (Tussah), 609 (Ecru), 610 (Dk Ecru), 612 (Lt Amethyst), 621 (Lt French Blue), 625 (Lt Beige), 884 (Shaded Pink), 889 (Shaded Lavender), 897 (Shaded Yellow).

White, 609 (Ecru) and 610 (Dk Ecru) are also available in ticket No.3, 5, 10 and 40. For larger articles this may be a more economical purchase. It is advisable to purchase at one time the number of balls sufficient for your requirements.

Colour variations
While the colour in this book has been reproduced as accurately as possible, slight variations can be expected between the printed representation and the actual worked design.

*Asterisk
Repeat instructions following the asterisk as many more times as specified in addition to the original.

Repeat instructions in parentheses as many times as specified. For example, '(1 hlf tr into next sp, 9 ch) 9 times', means to make all that is in parentheses 9 times in all.

Tension
Check this carefully before commencing your design as only the correct tension will ensure the best finished specimens. If your work is loose use a size finer hook/needle, if tight use a size larger hook/needle.

Sewing thread recommendation
When making up or finishing articles by hand or by machine, use the multi-purpose sewing thread Coats *Drima* (polyester). This thread is fine, yet very strong and is obtainable in a wide range of shades. Fine/ Medium Fabrics, eg Linen or Cotton use Machine Needle No.14 (British) 90 (Continental); No. of stitches to the cm (in.) 4–5 (10–12); Milward Hand Needle No.7 or 8.

Laundering
Mercer-Crochet colours are fast dyed and are highly resistant to even the most severe washing treatments but these colours may be adversely affected when washed in certain commercial washing preparations which contain high levels of fluorescent brightening (whitening) agents. To maintain the true tones of Mercer-Crochet colours it is recommended that pure soap flakes type washing agents be used as these generally contain only low concentrations of fluorescent brightening (whitening) agents.

Items should not be washed when work is still in progress. The assembled article should be washed on completion.

Make a warm lather of pure soap flakes and wash in the usual way, either by hand or washing machine. If desired, the article may be spin-dried until it is damp, or left until it is half dry. Place a piece of paper, either plain white or squared, on top of a clean, flat board. Following the correct measurements, draw the shape of the finished article on to the paper, using ruler and set square for squares and rectangles and a pair of compasses for circles. Using rustless pins, pin the work out to the pencilled shape, taking care not to strain the article. Pin out the general shape first, then finish by pinning each picot, loop or space into position. Special points to note carefully when pinning out are:

(a) When pinning loops, make sure the pin is in the centre of each loop to form balanced lines.
(b) When pinning scallops, make all the scallops the same size and regularly curved.
(c) Pull out all picots.
(d) Where there are flowers, pull out each petal in position.
(e) When pinning filet crochet, make sure that the spaces and blocks are square and that all edges are even and straight.

If the work requires to be slightly stiffened, use a solution of starch – 1 dessertspoonful to $\frac{1}{2}$ litre (1 pint) hot water, and dab lightly over the article. Raise the article up off the paper, to prevent it sticking as it dries. When dry, remove the pins and press the article lightly with a hot iron.

Metric measurements

As designers are now working in the metric system, it is only possible to provide pattern instructions with complete accuracy in metric measurements. In this book we give approximate Imperial measurement equivalents in brackets after the metric size where we feel they are still useful, ie in setting out fabric widths in the materials required and in indicating an approximate size for the finished article.

For readers who still prefer to work in Imperial measurements, a brief comparison guide is given for shorter measurements; for longer measurements, the easiest way to convert is to use a tape measure showing inches and centimetres, *but it should be stressed that for best results only the metric measurements should be used.*

COMPARISON GUIDE FOR SHORT MEASUREMENTS
(APPROXIMATE)

1	cm =	$\frac{3}{8}$ in.	35 cm =	$13\frac{3}{4}$ in.
1.5 cm =		$\frac{5}{8}$ in.	40 cm =	$15\frac{3}{4}$ in.
2	cm =	$\frac{3}{4}$ in.	45 cm =	$17\frac{3}{4}$ in.
2.5 cm =		1 in.	50 cm =	$19\frac{3}{4}$ in.
5	cm =	2 in.	55 cm =	$21\frac{5}{8}$ in.
7.5 cm =		3 in.	60 cm =	$23\frac{5}{8}$ in.
10	cm =	4 in.	65 cm =	$25\frac{5}{8}$ in.
12.5 cm =		5 in.	70 cm =	$27\frac{1}{2}$ in.
15	cm =	6 in.	75 cm =	$29\frac{1}{2}$ in.
17.5 cm =		$6\frac{7}{8}$ in.	80 cm =	$31\frac{1}{2}$ in.
20	cm =	$7\frac{7}{8}$ in.	85 cm =	$33\frac{1}{2}$ in.
22.5 cm =		$8\frac{7}{8}$ in.	90 cm =	$35\frac{1}{2}$ in.
25	cm =	$9\frac{7}{8}$ in.	95 cm =	$37\frac{3}{8}$ in.
27.5 cm =		$10\frac{7}{8}$ in.	100 cm =	$39\frac{3}{8}$ in.
30	cm =	$11\frac{3}{4}$ in.	(1 metre)

Buying fabrics

LENGTH (APPROXIMATE)

10 cm =	4 in.
20 cm =	$7\frac{7}{8}$ in.
30 cm =	$11\frac{3}{4}$ in.
40 cm =	$15\frac{3}{4}$ in.
50 cm =	$19\frac{3}{4}$ in.
60 cm =	$23\frac{5}{8}$ in.
70 cm =	$27\frac{1}{2}$ in.
80 cm =	$31\frac{1}{2}$ in.
90 cm =	$35\frac{1}{2}$ in.
1 m =	$39\frac{3}{8}$ in.

CROCHET

Introduction

The art of crochet is very old indeed, but from the details available it has never been possible to give any accurate information as to its history. It would appear to have been associated with France, as its name is in fact the French word for hook, and a small hook is used in the making of crochet lace. During the sixteenth century a considerable amount of crochet was produced in the convents of Europe. Without doubt it was the nuns who carried the craft to Ireland. There it was developed into quite an elaborate and distinctive form of rosettes, leaves and lace fillings.

During the time of Victoria this gentle craft was greatly abused. One can remember with horror the pictures of the overcrowded and overembellished drawing-rooms, complete with heavy crochet anti-macassars, mantlepiece covers with a fringing of clumsy bobbles and numerous other crochet pieces.

It was some years after the Victorian period that designers realized the potentialities of the craft, and crochet was revived with designs suitable for contemporary trends.

In the home, crochet lace can be used to make tablecloths, tray cloths and runners, and edgings from heavy to fine can fulfil a variety of functions.

The art of crochet is not difficult and it is reasonably quick to work. In the following pages simple diagrams and instructions are given to enable the beginner to master all the essential crochet stitches. From these a selection of designs are included which show the use of the individual stitches. Finally, notes and designs are included on all the various styles of crochet – motifs, all-over patterns, pineapple, filet, hairpin and Irish crochet.

Crochet stitches

Right-hand workers
Stitch diagrams. The shading on each stitch diagram denotes the foundation chain stitches and the number of turning chain stitches used at the end of the row.

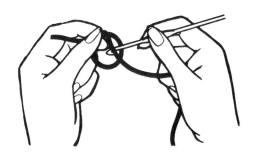

2
With right hand take hold of broad bar of hook as you would a pencil. Insert hook through loop and under yarn. With right hand, catch long end of yarn.

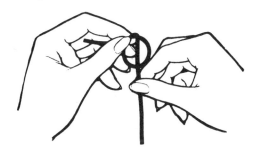

1   Position of thread and hook
Grasp yarn near one end of ball between thumb and forefinger of left hand. With right hand form yarn into loop. Hold loop in place between thumb and forefinger of left hand.

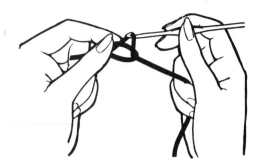

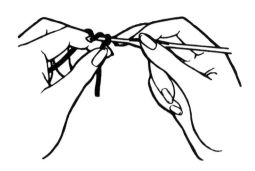

3

Draw loop through but do not remove hook from yarn. Pull short end in opposite direction to bring loop close round the end of the hook.

6

Pass your hook under yarn and catch yarn with hook. This is called 'yarn over'. Draw yarn through loop on hook. This makes one chain.

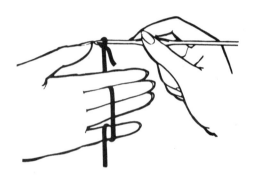

4

Loop yarn round little finger, across palm and behind forefinger of left hand. Grasp hook and loop between thumb and forefinger of left hand. Pull yarn gently so that it lies round the fingers firmly.

7   Chain – ch

This is the foundation of crochet work. With yarn in position and the loop on the hook as shown in diagram 5, pass the hook under the yarn held in left hand and catch yarn with hook (diagram 7), draw yarn through loop on hook, repeat this movement until chain is desired length (diagram 8).

8

5

Catch knot of loop between thumb and forefinger. Hold broad bar of hook with right hand as described in diagram 2.

9   Slip stitch – ss
Insert hook into stitch to left of hook, catch yarn with
hook and draw through stitch and loop on hook.

13   Half treble – hlf tr
Pass hook under the yarn held in left hand (diagram
13), insert hook into 3rd stitch to left of hook, yarn
over hook and draw through stitch (3 loops on hook),
yarn over hook (diagram 14), draw yarn through all
loops on hook (1 loop remains on hook) (diagram 15).
Continue working into each stitch to left of hook.

10

14

11

12

15

10   Double crochet – dc
Insert hook into 2nd stitch to left of hook, catch yarn
with hook (diagram 10) draw through stitch (2 loops
on hook) (diagram 11), yarn over hook and draw
through 2 loops on hook (1 loop remains on hook)
(diagram 12). Continue working into each stitch to
left of hook.

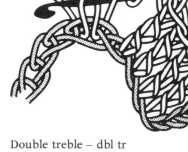

16 Treble – tr

Pass hook under the yarn of left hand (diagram 16), insert hook into 4th stitch to left of hook, yarn over hook and draw through stitch (3 loops on hook), yarn over hook (diagram 17), and draw through 2 loops on hook, yarn over hook (diagram 18), and draw through remaining 2 loops (1 loop remains on hook) (diagram 19). Continue working into each stitch to left of hook.

20 Double treble – dbl tr

Pass hook under the yarn of left hand twice, insert hook into 5th stitch to left of hook, yarn over hook and draw through stitch (4 loops on hook) (diagram 20), yarn over hook and draw through 2 loops on hook, yarn over hook and draw through other 2 loops on hook, yarn over hook and draw through remaining 2 loops (1 loop remains on hook). Continue working into each stitch to left of hook.

17

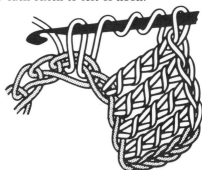

21 Triple treble – trip tr

Pass hook under the yarn of left hand 3 times, insert hook into 6th stitch to left of hook, yarn over hook and draw through stitch (5 loops on hook) (diagram 21), yarn over hook and draw through 2 loops on hook, (yarn over hook and draw through other 2 loops on hook) 3 times (1 loop remains on hook). Continue working into each stitch to left of hook.

18

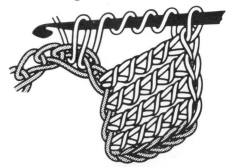

22 Quadruple treble – quad tr

Pass hook under the yarn of left hand 4 times, insert hook into 7th stitch to left of hook and complete in same manner as trip tr until only 1 loop remains.

19

23 Space(s) – sp(s)
Filet Crochet
The following four stitches are used mostly in Filet Crochet and are referred to as spaces and blocks, lacets and bars.

Spaces may be made with 2 ch, miss 2 stitches, 1 tr into next stitch.

26 Picot – p
Make a ch of 3, 4 or 5 stitches according to length of picot desired, then join ch to form a ring by working 1 dc into first ch.

24 Block(s) – blk(s) and space (sp)
1 tr into 4th stitch to left of hook, 1 tr into each of next 2 stitches, 2 ch, miss 2 stitches, 1 tr into next stitch, 1 tr into each of next 3 stitches.

27 Cluster(s) – cl(s)
Leaving the last loop of each on hook, work 2, 3 or more tr or dbl tr into same stitch, yarn over hook and draw through all loops on hook.

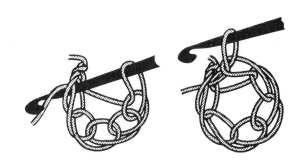

25 Bar and lacet
(a) A bar consists of 5 ch, miss 5 stitches or a lacet, 1 tr into next stitch.
(b) A lacet consists of 3 ch, miss 2 stitches, 1 dc into next stitch, 3 ch, miss 2 stitches, 1 tr into next stitch.

28 Joining circle with a slip stitch
Make a ch of 6 stitches. Join with a ss into first ch to form a ring.

29 Popcorn stitch

1 ch, 5 tr into next stitch, remove loop from hook, insert hook into 1 ch before group of treble then into dropped loop and draw it through.

30 Solomon's knot

Draw a loop on hook out 6 mm ($\frac{1}{4}$ in.), yarn over hook and draw through loop on hook. Insert hook between loop and single thread of this ch and make a dc. Work another knot in same manner (1 Solomon's Knot made), miss 4 stitches, 1 dc into next stitch. Repeat from beginning to end of row. Make $1\frac{1}{2}$ Solomon's Knot to turn, 1 dc over double loop at right of first centre knot of preceding row, 1 dc over double loop at left of same knot, 1 Solomon's Knot. Repeat to end of row.

31 Puff stitch

Commence with a length of ch having a multiple of 2 ch plus 1. 1st Row: 1 tr into 4th ch from hook, * yarn over hook, insert hook into next ch and draw yarn up 1 cm ($\frac{3}{8}$ in.) (yarn over hook, insert hook into same ch and draw yarn up as before) 3 times, yarn over and draw through all loops on hook (a puff st made), 1 ch, miss 1 ch; repeat from * to last 3 ch, a puff st into next ch, 1 tr into each of next 2 ch, 3 ch, turn.

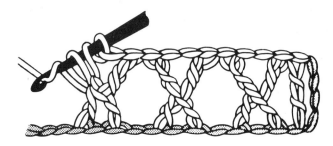

32 Crossed treble

Commence with a length of ch, having a multiple of 4 ch plus 2. 1st Row: 1 dbl tr into 5th ch from hook, * yarn over hook twice, insert hook into next ch and draw yarn through, yarn over hook and draw through 2 loops, yarn over hook, miss 1 ch, insert hook into next ch and draw yarn through, (yarn over hook and draw through 2 loops) 4 times, 1 ch, 1 tr into centre point of cross (cross completed), 1 ch, miss 1 ch; repeat from * to last 2 ch, 1 dbl tr into each of next 2 ch, 4 ch, turn.

How to 'Turn your Work'

In rows of crochet a certain number of chain stitches are added at the end of each row to bring the work into position for the next row. Then the work is turned so that the reverse side is facing the worker. The number of turning chain depends upon the stitch with which you intend to begin the next row.

TURNING CHAIN	
dc	1 ch
hlf tr	2 ch
tr	3 ch ⎫
dbl tr	4 ch ⎪
trip tr	5 ch ⎬
quad tr	6 ch ⎪
quin tr	7 ch ⎭

The list above gives the number of turning ch for each type of stitch which would be used when the following row is to be commenced with the same stitch. When applied to any of the stitches bracketed, the turning ch also stands as the first stitch of the next row.

1 Position of thread and hook
Grasp yarn near one end of ball between thumb and forefinger of right hand. With left hand form yarn into loop. Hold loop in place between thumb and forefinger of right hand.

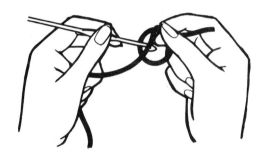

2
With left hand take hold of broad bar of hook as you would a pencil. Insert hook through loop and under yarn. With left hand, catch long end of yarn.

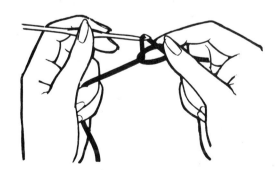

3
Draw loop through but do not remove hook from yarn. Pull short end in opposite direction to bring loop close round the end of the hook.

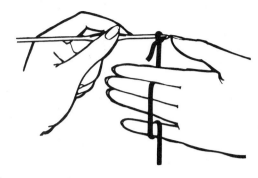

4
Loop yarn round little finger, across palm and behind forefinger of right hand. Grasp hook and loop between thumb and forefinger of right hand. Pull yarn gently so that it lies round the fingers firmly.

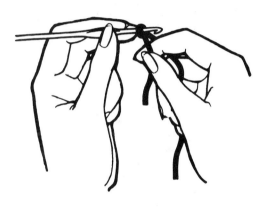

5
Catch knot of loop between thumb and forefinger. Hold broad bar of hook with left hand as described in diagram 2.

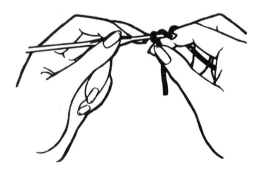

6
Pass your hook under yarn and catch yarn with hook. This is called 'yarn over'. Draw yarn through loop on hook. This makes one chain.

For stages 7 to 32, place a pocket mirror to the left of illustrations 7–32 (pages 10–14) to see the construction of the stitch in the mirror.

Crochet Hooks

These are the correct numbers of steel hooks to use with Coats Mercer-Crochet:

MERCER-CROCHET	MILWARD STEEL CROCHET HOOK
No.3 ⎫ No.5 ⎭	1.75 (no.2)
No.10 ⎫ No.15 ⎭	1.50 (no.2½)
No.20 ⎫ No.30 ⎭	1.25 (no.3)
No.40 ⎫ No.50 ⎭	1.00 (no.4)
No.60 ⎫ No.70 ⎭	0.75 (no.5)
No.80	0.60 (no.6)

British/American equivalents

The following tables show the nearest equivalent sizes of American crochet hooks/knitting needles. Before commencing an article work a tension sample and adjust hook/needle size accordingly. (See paragraph on 'Tension'.)

CROCHET HOOKS

British	American
0.60 (no.6)	14
	13
0.75 (no.5)	12
	11
1.00 (no.4)	10
	9
1.25 (no.3)	8
1.50 (no.2½)	7
	6
	5
1.75 (no.2)	4
	3
	2
2.00 (no.1)	1

KNITTING NEEDLES

British	American
2 (no.14)	0
2¼ (no.13)	1
2½ (nos 13/12)	
2¾ (no.12)	2
3 (no.11)	
3¼ (no.10)	3

Abbreviations

ch – chain; dc – double crochet– hlf tr – half treble; tr – treble; dbl tr – double treble; trip tr – triple treble; quad tr – quadruple treble; quin tr – quintuple treble; ss – slip stitch; st(s) ; stitch(es); sp(s) – space(s); blk – block. ☐ space ■ block.

British/American equivalents

British	American
ch (chain)	ch (chain)
dc (double crochet)	sc (single crochet)
hlf tr (half treble)	half dc (half double crochet)
tr (treble)	dc (double crochet)
dbl tr (double treble)	tr (treble)
trip tr (triple treble)	dbl tr (double treble)
quad tr (quadruple treble)	trip tr (triple treble)
ss (slip stitch)	sl st (slip stitch)

HAIRPIN LACE

How to work the lace

Use a crochet hook and hairpin lace staple. Hold the crochet hook in the right hand. Make a loop at end of ball thread and slip on to crochet hook. Take the hairpin in the left hand and hold it flat between the thumb and first finger, with prong end uppermost and the round part downwards in the palm of the hand. (See Steps 1 to 7.)

Step 1 Make a loop at end of ball thread (diagram 1).
Step 2 Insert hook in loop and wind ball thread around right prong of hairpin (diagram 1).
Step 3 Thread over hook and draw through loop, keeping loop at centre (diagram 1).

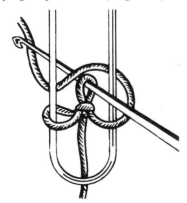

Step 4 Raise hook to a vertical position and turn hairpin to the left (diagram 2).

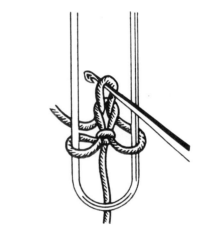

Step 5 Thread over hook and draw through loop on hook (diagram 3).

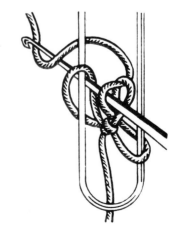

Step 6 Insert hook into loop of left prong (diagram 4).
Step 7 Thread over hook and draw loop through (2 loops on hook), thread over and draw through remaining 2 loops.
Repeat steps 4 to 7 for length required.

CROCHET MOTIFS

Many and varied are the motif designs in modern crochet. Their shape may be based on the square, the circle or the hexagon. They may be joined together in groups to form an all-over lace or the joining may be achieved by separate crochet sections known as 'fillings'. The introduction of a filling is part of the design plan.

Motifs are a most adaptable form of crochet design. Joined together as a border they may trim the edges of tea cloths, runners and chair-backs. If crocheted to form an all-over lace pattern, they can be made to form luncheon mats, tray cloths, runners, chairbacks, cheval sets and tea cloths.

Interesting effects can be developed by the use of two colours of Mercer-Crochet, either by a check pattern or by rows of alternate borders.

Round Cushion (see plate 1 page 25)

Coats Chain Mercer-Crochet Cotton No.20 (20 g).
1 ball each of 687 (Tangerine), 962 (Dk Buttercup), 513 (Orange) and 442 (Mid Buttercup).
This model is worked in these four shades, but any other shades of Mercer-Crochet may be used.
Milward steel crochet hook 1.25 (no.3).
1.30 m green furnishing fabric 122 cm (approximately 48 in.) wide.
2 m piping cord.

Tension
First motif – 9 cm ($3\frac{5}{8}$ in.) from point to point.
Second motif – 6.5 cm ($2\frac{5}{8}$ in.) from point to point.
Third motif – 3.8 cm ($1\frac{1}{2}$ in.) in diameter.
Fourth motif – 2.8 cm ($1\frac{1}{8}$ in.) in diameter.
Fifth motif – 1.5 cm ($\frac{5}{8}$ in.) in diameter.

Measurements
56 cm (22 in.) in diameter.

First motif (make 5)
Using Tangerine commence with 12 ch, join with a ss to form a ring.
1st Row: 3 ch, 4 tr into ring, remove loop from hook, insert hook into 3rd of 3 ch and draw dropped loop through (a starting popcorn st made), * 3 ch, 5 tr into ring, remove loop from hook, insert hook into first tr of tr group and draw dropped loop through (another popcorn st made); repeat from * 6 times more ending with 3 ch, 1 ss into first popcorn st.
2nd Row: 1 ss into first loop, 1 dc into same loop, * 5 ch, 1 dc into next loop; repeat from * ending with 5 ch, 1 ss into first dc.
3rd Row: 1 ss into first loop, 3 ch, 6 tr into same loop, 7 tr into each loop, 1 ss into 3rd of 3 ch.
4th Row: * 1 dc into next tr, 5 ch, miss 3 tr, 1 dc into next tr, 3 ch, miss 2 tr; repeat from * omitting 3 ch at end of last repeat, 1 ch, 1 hlf tr into first dc.
5th Row: 1 dc into loop just made, * 7 ch, leaving the last loop of each on hook work 4 trip tr into next 5 ch loop, thread over and draw through all loops on hook (a cluster made), 4 ch, 1 ss into top of cluster (a picot made), 7 ch, 1 dc into next 3 ch loop; repeat from * omitting 1 dc at end of last repeat, 1 ss into first dc. Fasten off.
6th Row: Attach thread to any picot, 1 dc into same place as join, * 13 ch, 1 dc into next picot; repeat from * ending with 13 ch, 1 ss into first dc.
7th row: * Into next loop work (1 dc 1 hlf tr 1 tr 4 dbl tr 1 tr 1 hlf tr) twice and 1 dc; repeat from * ending with 1 ss into first dc. Fasten off.

Second motif (make 5)
Using Dk Buttercup work as first motif for 5 rows. Fasten off.

Third motif (make 5)
Using Orange work as first motif for 3 rows. Fasten off.

Fourth motif (make 5)
Using Mid Buttercup work as first motif for 1 row.
2nd Row: 1 ss into first loop, a starting popcorn st into same loop, * 5 ch, a popcorn st into next loop; repeat from * ending with 5 ch, 1 ss into first popcorn st. Fasten off.

Fifth motif (make 10)
Using Mid Buttercup work as first motif for 1 row. Fasten off. Damp and pin out to measurements.

To make up
1.5 cm ($\frac{1}{2}$ in.) seam allowance has been given on all pieces. Cut 2 circles from fabric 59 cm (23 in.) in diameter and 1 strip 9×178 cm ($3\frac{1}{2} \times 70$ in.) for gusset.

Using guide for position sew crochet in place to one circle for front of cushion. Cut and join sufficient bias strips to fit circumference of circle. Cover piping cord with bias strips. Baste and stitch. Baste piping cord to front of cushion, right sides together, edges even. Place gusset in position over piping cord. Baste and

stitch close to cord. Place other circle to remaining side of gusset. Baste and stitch leaving an opening. Trim seams and turn to right side. Insert pad and sew opening.

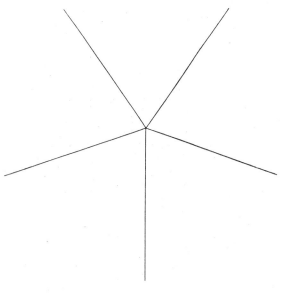

19

Square Cushion (see plate 2 page 26)

Coats Chain Mercer-Crochet Cotton No.20 (20 g).
3 balls 203 (Lido Blue) and 4 balls White. This model is worked in these two shades, but any other shades of Mercer-Crochet may be used.
Milward steel crochet hook 1.25 (no.3).
Cushion pad 40.5 cm (16 in.) square in contrasting colour.

Tension
Size of motif – 7.5 cm (3 in.) square.

Measurements
40.5 cm (16 in.) square including edging.

First motif
Using Lido Blue commence with 6 ch, join with a ss to form a ring.
1st Row: 12 dc into ring, 1 ss into back loop of first dc.
2nd Row: 1 dc into same place as ss, * 3 ch, 1 dc into back loop of next dc; repeat from * ending with 1 ss into first dc.
3rd Row: 1 ss into first loop, 3 ch, 5 tr into same loop, remove loop from hook, insert hook into 3rd of 3 ch and draw dropped loop through (a starting popcorn st made), * 3 ch, 6 tr into next loop, remove loop from hook, insert hook into first tr of tr group and draw dropped loop through (a popcorn st made); repeat from * ending with 3 ch, 1 ss into first popcorn st.
4th Row: 1 dc into same place as ss, * into next loop work 1 dc 13 ch 1 dc into 2nd ch from hook 1 dc into each of next 11 ch and 1 dc – a spoke made – 1 dc into next popcorn st, (into next loop work 1 dc 10 ch 1 dc into 2nd ch from hook 1 dc into each of next 8 ch and 1 dc – another spoke made – 1 dc into next popcorn st) twice; repeat from * omitting 1 dc at end of last repeat, 1 ss into first dc. Fasten off.
5th Row: With right side facing attach White to same place as last ss, 13 ch, * 1 dc into tip of next spoke, 9 ch, miss 1 dc after spoke, 1 dbl tr into next dc, (6 ch, 1 dc into tip of next spoke, 6 ch, miss 1 dc after spoke, 1 dbl tr into next dc) twice, 9 ch; repeat from * omitting 1 dbl tr and 9 ch at end of last repeat, 1 ss into 4th of 13 ch.
6th Row: * Into next loop work 1 dc 1 hlf tr and 9 tr, 1 tr into next dc, 3 ch, 1 ss into top of last tr – a picot made – into next loop work 9 tr 1 hlf tr and 1 dc (into next loop work 1 dc 1 hlf tr and 6 tr, 1 tr into next dc, a picot, into next loop work 6 tr 1 hlf tr and 1 dc) twice; repeat from * ending with 1 ss into first dc. Fasten off.

Centre
With right side facing attach White to front loop of first dc on 1st row, 1 dc into same place as join, * 3 ch, 1 dc into front loop of next dc; repeat from * ending with 3 ch, 1 ss into first dc.

Second motif
Work as first motif for 5 rows.
6th Row: Into next loop work 1 dc 1 hlf tr and 9 tr, 1 tr into next dc, 1 ch, 1 ss into corresponding picot on first motif, 1 ch, 1 ss into top of last tr on second motif, into next loop work 9 tr 1 hlf tr and 1 dc, (into next loop work 1 dc 1 hlf tr and 6 tr, 1 tr into next dc, 1 ch, 1 ss into next picot on first motif, 1 ch, 1 ss into top of last tr on second motif, into next loop work 6 tr 1 hlf tr and 1 dc) twice, into next loop work 1 dc 1 hlf tr and 9 tr, 1 tr into next dc, 1 ch, 1 ss into next picot on first motif, 1 ch, 1 ss into top of last tr on second motif and complete as first motif.
Make 5 rows of 5 motifs joining each as second motif was joined to first. Where 4 corners meet join 3rd and 4th motifs to joining of previous motifs.
Make another section to correspond.
Damp and pin out to measurements.

Joining
1st Row: Place wrong side of sections together and working through both sections attach White to picot at any corner, into same place as join work 1 dc 7 ch and 1 dc (a corner loop made), * 13 ch, 1 dc into next picot, 9 ch, 1 dc into next picot, 13 ch, 1 dc into next join of motifs; repeat from * to within last motif along side, 13 ch, 1 dc into next picot, 9 ch, 1 dc into next picot, 13 ch, into next picot work 1 dc 7 ch and 1 dc (another corner loop made); repeat from first * twice more, continuing to work along one section only repeat from first * once more omitting a corner loop at end of repeat, 1 ss into first dc.
2nd Row: 1 dc into same place as ss, ** into next loop work 1 dc 1 hlf tr 3 tr a picot 2 tr 1 hlf tr and 1 dc, 1 dc into next dc, * into next loop work 1 dc 1 hlf tr 6 tr a picot 5 tr 1 hlf tr and 1 dc, 1 dc into next dc, into next loop work 1 dc 1 hlf tr 4 tr a picot 3 tr 1 hlf tr and 1 dc, 1 dc into next dc, into next loop work 1 dc 1 hlf tr 6 tr a picot 5 tr 1 hlf tr and 1 dc, 1 dc into next dc; repeat from * to within next corner loop; repeat from ** 3 times more omitting 1 dc at end of last repeat, 1 ss into first dc. Fasten off. Damp and pin out to measurements.
Insert pad and sew opening.

Motif Tablecloth (see plate 3 page 27)

Coats Chain Mercer-Crochet Cotton No.20 (20 g).
25 balls. This model is worked in shade 787 (Lt Moss
Green), but any other shade of Mercer-Crochet may
be used.
Milward steel crochet hook 1.25 (no.3).

Tension
Size of motif – 8.8 cm (3½ in.) square.

Measurements
114.5 cm (45 in.) square approximately.

First motif
Commence with 16 ch, join with a ss to form a ring.
1st Row: 3 ch, 35 tr into ring, 1 ss into 3rd of 3 ch.
2nd Row: 1 dc into same place as ss, * 3 ch, miss 2 tr,
1 dc into next tr; repeat from * ending with 3 ch, 1 ss
into first dc.
3rd Row: 1 ss into next loop, 3 ch, 5 tr into same loop,
remove loop from hook, insert hook into 3rd of 3 ch
and draw dropped loop through (a starting popcorn
st made), 3 ch, 1 dbl tr into same loop, 3 ch, 6 tr into
same loop, remove loop from hook, insert hook into
first tr of tr group and draw dropped loop through
(a popcorn st made), * (3 ch, 1 dc into next loop) twice,
3 ch, into next loop work a popcorn st 3 ch 1 dbl tr
3 ch and a popcorn st; repeat from * ending with
(3 ch, 1 dc into next loop) twice, 3 ch, 1 ss into first
popcorn st.
4th Row: 1 ss into next sp, 3 ch, a starting popcorn st
into same sp, * 3 ch, into next dbl tr work 1 dbl tr 5 ch

and 1 dbl tr, (3 ch, a popcorn st into next sp) 5 times;
repeat from * omitting a popcorn st at end of last
repeat, 1 ss into first popcorn st.
5th Row: 1 ss into next sp, 3 ch, 2 tr into same sp,
* 1 tr into next dbl tr, into next sp work 3 tr 3 ch and
3 tr, 1 tr into next dbl tr, (3 tr into next sp) 6 times;
repeat from * omitting 3 tr at end of last repeat, 1 ss
into 3rd of 3 ch.
6th Row: 1 ss into each of next 6 tr and into sp, into
same sp work 1 dc 10 ch and 1 dc, * (10 ch, miss 8 tr,
1 dc into next tr) twice, 10 ch, into next sp work 1 dc
10 ch and 1 dc; repeat from * omitting 1 dc 10 ch and
1 dc at end of last repeat, 1 ss into first dc.
7th Row: Into each loop work 1 dc 1 hlf tr 4 tr 3 ch
1 dc into last tr – a picot made – 3 tr 1 hlf tr and 1 dc,
1 ss into first dc. Fasten off.

Second motif
Work as first motif for 6 rows.
7th Row: Into next loop work 1 dc 1 hlf tr and 4 tr,
1 ch, 1 dc into corresponding picot on first motif,
1 ch, 1 dc into last tr made on second motif, into same
loop work 3 tr 1 hlf tr and 1 dc, (into next loop work
1 dc 1 hlf tr and 4 tr, 1 ch, 1 dc into next picot on first
motif, 1 ch, 1 dc into last tr made on second motif,
into same loop work 3 tr 1 hlf tr and 1 dc) 4 times and
complete as first motif.
Make 13 rows of 13 motifs joining each as second
motif was joined to first. Where 4 corners meet join
3rd and 4th motifs to joining of previous motifs.
Damp and pin out to measurements.

ALL-OVER PATTERNS

This section is devoted to all-over patterns. As can be seen on the following pages a large variety of articles can be produced from this type of pattern.

Glass Holders (see plate 4 page 28)

Coats Chain Mercer-Crochet Cotton No.20 (20 g).
1 ball each of shade 687 (Tangerine), 513 (Orange), 789 (Mid Moss Green), 579 (Brown), 602 (Lt Cream) and 795 (Amber Gold). This model is worked in these six shades, but any other shades of Mercer-Crochet may be used.
Milward steel crochet hook 1.25 (no.3).
3 holders may be worked from 1 ball.
6 glasses with base approximately 5.5 cm (2¼ in.) in diameter.

Tension
First 2 rows – 2 cm (¾ in.) in diameter.

Measurement
Depth of Holder – 5.5 cm (2¼ in.).

Base
Commence with 4 ch.
1st Row: 11 tr into 4th ch from hook, 1 ss into 4th of 4 ch.
2nd and **3rd Rows:** 3 ch, 1 tr into same place as ss, 2 tr into each tr, 1 ss into 3rd of 3 ch.
4th Row: 3 ch, 1 tr into same place as ss, * 1 tr into next tr, 2 tr into next tr; repeat from * ending with 1 tr into next tr, 1 ss into 3rd of 3 ch.
5th Row: 3 ch, 1 tr into same place as ss, * 1 tr into each of next 5 tr, 2 tr into next tr; repeat from * ending with 1 tr into each of next 5 tr, 1 ss into 3rd of 3 ch.

6th Row: 1 dc into same place as ss, 1 dc into each tr, 1 ss into first dc. (84 dc)

Side
1st Row: 1 dc into same place as ss, * 6 ch, miss 6 dc, 1 dc into next dc; repeat from * omitting 1 dc at end of last repeat, 1 ss into first dc.
2nd Row: Into each loop work 1 dc 1 hlf tr 7 tr 1 hlf tr and 1 dc, 1 ss into first dc.
3rd Row: 1 ss into each of next 4 sts, 1 dc into next tr, * 3 ch, 1 tr into 3rd ch from hook, miss 10 sts, leaving the last loop of each on hook work 3 dbl tr into next tr, thread over and draw through all loops on hook (a 3 dbl tr cluster made), 3 ch, 1 tr into 3rd ch from hook, into same tr work (a 3 dbl tr cluster 3 ch 1 tr into 3rd ch from hook) twice and a 3 dbl tr cluster, 3 ch, 1 tr into 3rd ch from hook, miss 10 sts, 1 dc into next tr; repeat from * omitting 1 dc at end of last repeat, 1 ss into first dc. Fasten off.

Strip
Commence with 7 ch.
1st Row: 1 quad tr into 7th ch from hook, * 6 ch, 1 quad tr into top of last quad tr; repeat from * 10 times more, 1 ss into first ch worked.
2nd and **3rd Rows:** As 2nd and 3rd rows of side.
4th Row: With right side facing, attach thread to first loop worked on opposite side of 1st row and work as 2nd row of side. *continued on page 41*

Plate 1   Working instructions on pages 18 and 19

Plate 2   Working instructions on page 20

Plate 3   Working instructions on page 22

Plate 4   Working instructions on pages 24 and 41

Plate 5   *Working instructions on page 42*

Plate 6   Working instructions on pages 52 to 54

Plate 7   Working instructions on pages 55 and 56

Plate 8   Working instructions on pages 57 and 58

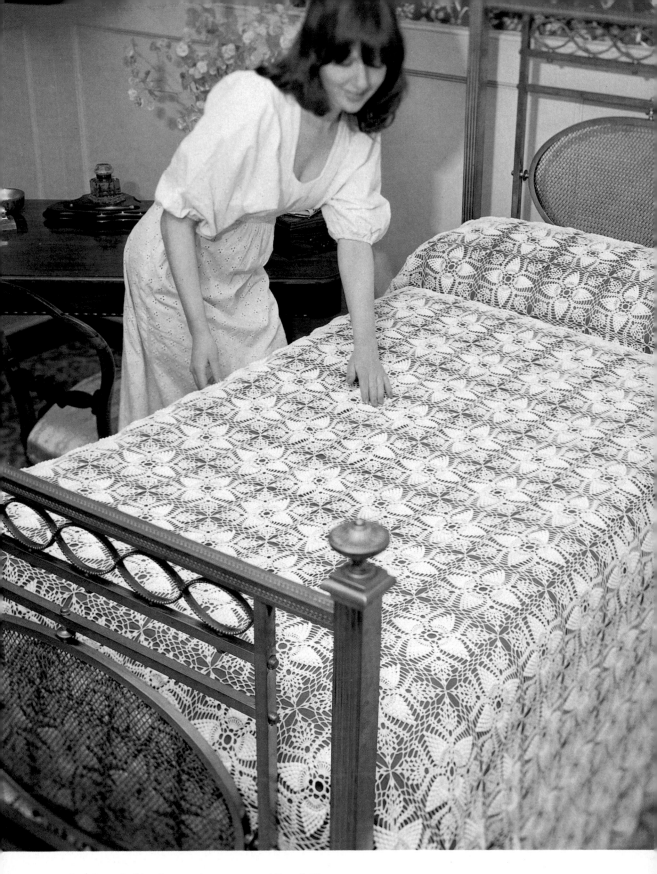

Plate 9   Working instructions on pages 59 and 60

Plate 10   Working instructions on pages 72 and 73

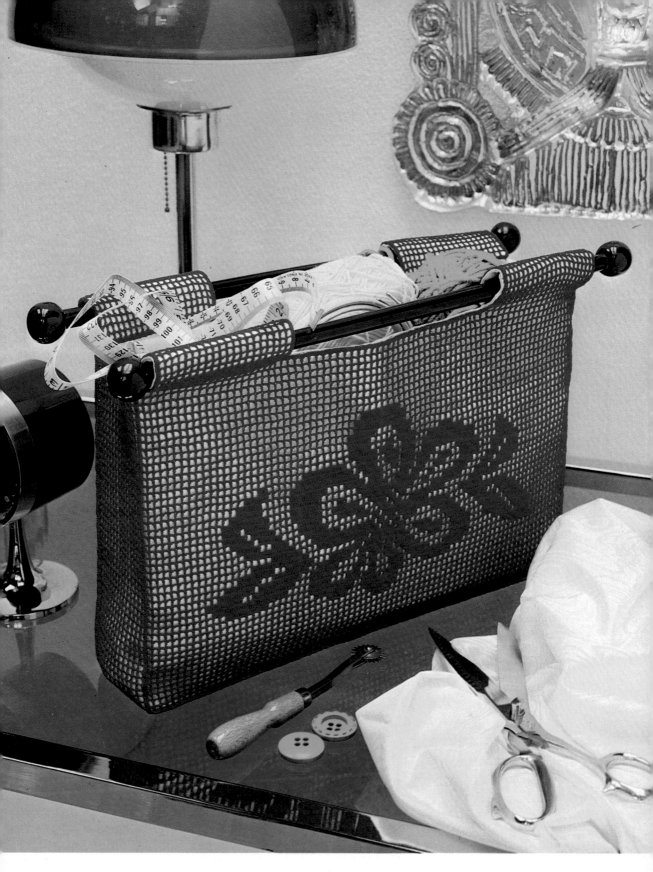

Plate 11   Working instructions on pages 73 to 75

Plate 12   Working instructions on pages 76 and 77

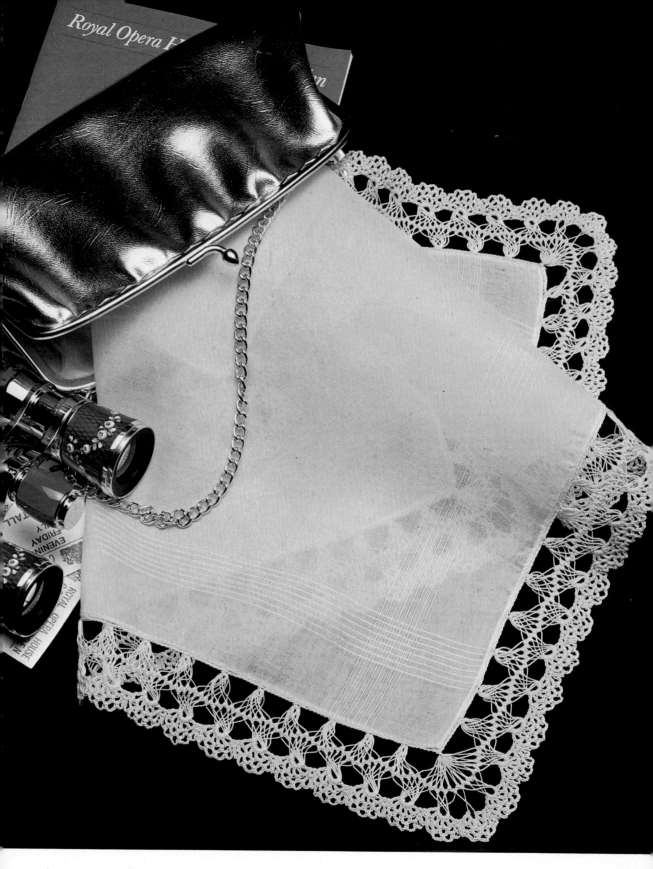

Plate 13   Working instructions on page 79

Plate 14   Working instructions on pages 83 and 84

Plate 15   Working instructions on pages 105 and 106

Plate 16   Working instructions on pages 107 and 108

5th Row: 1 ss into each of next 4 sts, 1 dc into next tr, * 3 ch, 1 tr into 3rd ch from hook, miss 10 sts, into next tr work a 3 dbl tr cluster 3 ch 1 tr into 3rd ch from hook and a 3 dbl tr cluster, 1 ch, 1 dc into corresponding loop on 3rd row of side, 1 ch, miss 2 sts, 1 tr into next ch (a joining made), into same tr on strip work a 3 dbl tr cluster 3 ch 1 tr into 3rd ch from hook and a 3 dbl tr cluster, 3 ch, 1 tr into 3rd ch from hook, miss 10 sts, 1 dc into next tr; repeat from * omitting 1 dc at end of last repeat, 1 ss into first dc. Fasten off.

Punch Set (see plate 5 page 29)

Coats Chain Mercer-Crochet Cotton No.20 (20 g).
2 balls. This model is worked in shade 513 (Orange), but any other shade of Mercer-Crochet may be used.
Milward steel crochet hook 1.25 (no.3).
1 circle of glass 20.5 cm (8 in.) in diameter.
6 circles of glass 11.5 cm ($4\frac{1}{2}$ in.) in diameter.

Tension
First 4 rows – 4.5 cm ($1\frac{3}{4}$ in.) in diameter.

Measurements
Small mat – 11.5 cm ($4\frac{1}{2}$ in.) in diameter.
Large mat – 20.5 cm (8 in.) in diameter.

Large mat
Commence with 8 ch, join with a ss to form a ring.
1st Row: 16 dc into ring, 1 ss into first dc.
2nd Row: 1 dc into same place as ss, * 7 ch, 1 dc into second ch from hook, 1 dc into each of next 3 ch (a spoke made), 2 ch, miss 1 dc on ring, 1 dc into next dc; repeat from * omitting 1 dc at end of last repeat, 1 ss into first dc.
3rd Row: Ss to tip of first spoke, 1 dc into same place as last ss, * 9 ch, 1 dc into tip of next spoke; repeat from * ending with 9 ch, 1 ss into first dc.
4th Row: 1 dc into same place as ss, * 9 dc into next loop, 1 dc into next dc; repeat from * ending with 9 dc into next loop, 1 ss into first dc.
5th Row: 3 ch, 1 tr into each dc, 1 ss into 3rd of 3 ch.
6th Row: * 1 dc into each of next 2 tr, 2 dc into next tr, 1 dc into each of next 3 tr, 2 dc into next tr, 1 dc into each of next 2 tr, 11 ch, miss 1 tr; repeat from * ending with 1 ss into first dc.
7th Row: 1 ss into each of next 2 dc, * 1 dc into each of next 5 dc, 17 tr into next loop, miss 3 dc; repeat from * ending with 1 ss into first dc.
8th Row: 1 dc into next dc, * into next dc work 1 dc 5 ch 1 dc 7 ch 1 dc 5 ch and 1 dc (a triple picot made), 1 dc into next dc, miss 1 dc, 1 dc into each of next 8 tr, a triple picot into next tr, 1 dc into each of next 8 tr, miss 1 dc, 1 dc into next dc; repeat from * omitting 1 dc at end of last repeat, 1 ss into first dc.
9th Row: Ss to centre picot on next triple picot, 12 ch, 1 trip tr into same picot, * 9 ch, 1 dc into centre picot on next triple picot, 9 ch, into centre picot on next triple picot work 1 trip tr 7 ch and 1 trip tr; repeat from * omitting 1 trip tr 7 ch and 1 trip tr at end of last repeat, 1 ss into 5th of 12 ch.
10th Row: 1 dc into same place as ss, * 6 dc into next loop, 1 dc into next trip tr, 9 dc into next loop, 1 dc into next dc, 9 dc into next loop, 1 dc into next trip tr, 7 dc into next loop, 1 dc into next trip tr, 9 dc into

next loop, 1 dc into next dc, 9 dc into next loop, 1 dc into next trip tr; repeat from * omitting 1 dc at end of last repeat, 1 ss into first dc.
11th Row: 3 ch, 1 tr into each dc, 1 ss into 3rd of 3 ch.
12th Row: 1 dc into same place as ss, 1 dc into each of next 18 tr, * 13 ch, miss 1 tr, 1 dc into each of next 19 tr; repeat from * ending with 13 ch, miss 1 tr, 1 ss into first dc.
13th Row: 1 ss into each of next 2 dc, * 1 dc into each of next 13 dc, 19 tr into next loop, miss 3 dc; repeat from * ending with 1 ss into first dc.
14th Row: * 1 dc into each of next 5 dc, a triple picot into next dc, 1 dc into each of next 5 dc, miss 1 dc, 1 dc into each of next 9 tr, a triple picot into next tr, 1 dc into each of next 9 tr, miss 1 dc; repeat from * ending with 1 ss into first dc.
15th Row: Ss to centre picot on next triple picot, 11 ch, 1 dbl tr into same picot, * 11 ch, 1 dc into centre picot on next triple picot, 11 ch, into centre picot on next triple picot work 1 dbl tr 7 ch and 1 dbl tr; repeat from * omitting 1 dbl tr 7 ch and 1 dbl tr at end of last repeat, 1 ss into 4th of 11 ch.
16th Row: 1 dc into same place as ss, 7 dc into next loop, 1 dc into next dbl tr, * 11 dc into next loop, 1 dc into next dc, 11 dc into next loop, 1 dc into next dbl tr, 7 dc into next loop, 1 dc into next dbl tr; repeat from * omitting 9 dc at end of last repeat, 1 ss into first dc.
17th Row: 1 dc into same place as ss, * 4 ch, miss 3 dc, 1 dc into next dc; repeat from * ending with 1 ch, 1 tr into first dc.
18th Row: 1 dc into loop just formed, * 4 ch, 1 dc into next loop; repeat from * ending with 1 ch, 1 tr into first dc.
19th Row: 1 dc into loop just formed, * 3 ch, 1 dc into next loop; repeat from * ending with 1 ch, 1 hlf tr into first dc.
20th Row: 1 dc into loop just formed, * 3 ch, 1 dc into next loop; repeat from * ending with 3 ch, 1 ss into first dc.
21st Row: * 3 dc into next loop, 2 dc into each of next 3 loops; repeat from * ending with 1 ss into first dc. Fasten off.

Small mat (make 6)
Work as large mat for 8 rows.
9th and 10th Rows: As 15th and 16th rows of large mat.
11th Row: 1 dc into same place as ss, * 3 ch, miss 3 dc, 1 dc into next dc; repeat from * ending with 1 ch, 1 hlf tr into first dc.
12th to 14th Row: As 19th to 21st row.
Damp and pin out to measurements.
Slip crochet over circles of glass.

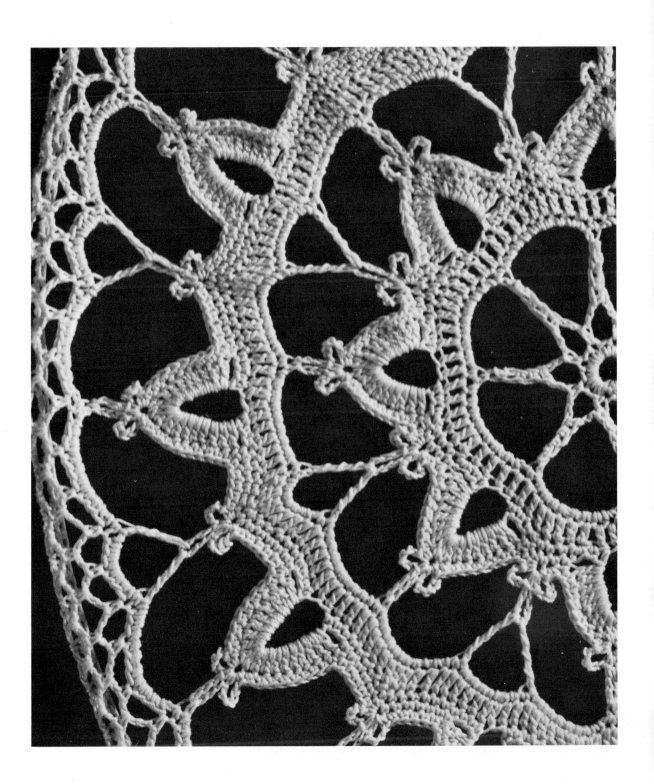

Lampshade Cover

Coats Chain Mercer-Crochet Cotton No.20 (20 g).
2 balls White, 1 ball 524 (Dk Jade) and 1 ball 789 (Mid Moss Green).
This model is worked in these three shades, but any other shades of Mercer-Crochet may be used.
Milward steel crochet hook 1.25 (no.3).
Lampshade 25 cm (9¾ in.) deep for covering.

Tension
First 5 rows – 2.5 cm (1 in.).
1 pattern – 5 cm (2 in.).

Measurements
25 × 66 cm (9¾ × 26 in.) adjustable.
Using White commence with 312 ch, or length required having a multiple of 24 ch. Being careful not to twist, join with a ss to form a ring.
1st Row: 1 dc into same place as ss, 1 dc into each ch, 1 ss into first dc.
2nd Row: 3 ch, into same place as ss work 1 tr 2 ch and 2 tr (a starting shell made), * 9 ch, miss 11 dc, into next dc work 1 tr 2 ch and 1 tr (a V st made), 9 ch, miss 11 dc, into next dc work 2 tr 2 ch and 2 tr (a shell made); repeat from * omitting a shell at end of last repeat, 1 ss into 3rd of 3 ch.
3rd Row: 1 ss into next tr, 1 ss into next sp, 3 ch, a starting shell into same sp, * 7 ch, 1 tr into first tr of V st, 1 ch, into sp of V st work (1 tr, 1 ch) twice and 1 tr, 1 ch, 1 tr into next tr, 7 ch, a shell into next shell; repeat from * omitting a shell at end of last repeat, 1 ss into 3rd of 3 ch.
4th Row: 1 ss into next tr, 1 ss into next sp, 3 ch, a starting shell into same sp, * 5 ch, miss 7 ch, (1 tr into next tr, 2 ch) 4 times, 1 tr into next tr, 5 ch, a shell into next shell; repeat from * omitting a shell at end of last repeat, 1 ss into 3rd of 3 ch.
5th Row: 1 ss into next tr, 1 ss into next sp, 3 ch, 4 tr into same sp, * 5 ch, miss 5 ch, 1 dc into next tr, (into next sp work 1 hlf tr 3 tr and 1 hlf tr, 1 dc into next tr) 4 times, 5 ch, 5 tr into next shell; repeat from * omitting 5 tr at end of last repeat, 1 ss into 3rd of 3 ch. Fasten off.
6th Row: Miss 1 tr, attach Dk Jade to next tr, 3 ch, a starting shell into same place as join, * 9 ch, miss 2 dc, 1 V st into next dc, 9 ch, a shell into centre tr of next treble group; repeat from * omitting a shell at end of last repeat, 1 ss into 3rd of 3 ch.
7th to 9th Row: As 3rd to 5th row.
10th Row: Miss 1 tr, attach White to next tr, 3 ch and complete as 6th row.
11th to 13th Row: As 3rd to 5th row.
14th Row: Miss 1 tr, attach Mid Moss Green to next tr, 3 ch and complete as 6th row.

15th to 17th Row: As 3rd to 5th row.
18th Row: As 10th row.
Repeat 3rd to 18th row once more or length required then 3rd to 13th row again. Do not fasten off.
Next Row: 1 ss into each of next 2 tr, 1 dc into same place as last ss, * 10 ch, miss 6 tr, 1 dc into next tr, 3 ch, miss 2 tr, 1 dc into next tr, 10 ch, miss 6 tr, 1 dc into next tr; repeat from * omitting 1 dc at end of last repeat, 1 ss into first dc.
Next Row: 1 dc into same place as ss, * 1 dc into each of next 10 ch, 1 dc into next dc, 1 dc into each of next 3 ch, 1 dc into next dc, 1 dc into each of next 10 ch, 1 dc into next dc; repeat from * omitting 1 dc at end of last repeat, 1 ss into first dc. Fasten off.
Damp and pin out to measurements.
Place crochet over lampshade and stitch in position.

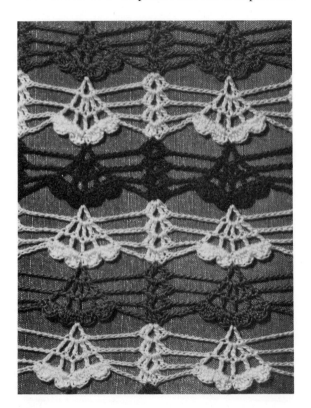

AFTER
EIGHT

Pin Cushion and Scissors Case

Coats Chain Mercer-Crochet Cotton No.20 (20 g).
1 ball. This model is worked in shade 524 (Dk Jade),
but any other shade of Mercer-Crochet may be used.
Milward steel crochet hook 1.25 (no.3).
25 cm fabric, 90 cm (approximately 36 in.) wide in
contrasting colour.
2 pieces of Vilene or other bonded fibre interlining,
12.5 × 7.5 cm (5 × 3 in.).
Kapok for stuffing pin cushion.
Coats *Drima* (polyester) thread.

Tension
First 2 rows – 2.5 cm (1 in.) in diameter.

Measurements
Pin cushion – 15 cm (6 in.) across widest part.
Scissors case – 14 cm (5½ in.) long.

Pin Cushion

Motif (make 2)
Commence with 8 ch, join with a ss to form a ring.
1st Row: 2 ch, leaving the last loop of each on hook
work 3 tr into ring, thread over and draw through all
loops on hook (a 3 tr cluster made), (3 ch, a 4 tr cluster
into ring) 5 times, 3 ch, 1 ss into first cluster.
2nd Row: 3 ch, * 5 tr into next sp, 1 tr into next
cluster; repeat from * ending with 5 tr into next sp,
1 ss into 3rd of 3 ch.
3rd Row: 1 ss into each of next 2 tr, 3 ch, into same
place as last ss work 2 tr 3 ch and 3 tr, * 5 ch, miss 4 tr,
1 dc into each of next 3 tr, 5 ch, miss 4 tr, into next tr
work 3 tr 3 ch and 3 tr (a shell made); repeat from *
omitting a shell at end of last repeat, 1 ss into 3rd of
3 ch.
4th Row: 1 ss into each of next 2 tr and into next sp,
3 ch, into same sp work 2 tr 3 ch and 3 tr, * 4 ch, 1 dc
into next loop, 12 ch, 1 dc into next loop, 4 ch, a shell
into sp of next shell; repeat from * omitting a shell at
end of last repeat, 1 ss into 3rd of 3 ch.
5th Row: 1 ss into each of next 2 tr and into next sp,
3 ch, into same sp work 2 tr 3 ch and 3 tr, * 4 ch, miss
1 sp, into next loop work (1 dbl tr, 1 ch) 9 times and
1 dbl tr, 4 ch, a shell into next shell; repeat from *
omitting a shell at end of last repeat, 1 ss into 3rd of
3 ch.
6th Row: 1 ss into each of next 2 sts and into next sp,
1 dc into same sp, * 5 ch, (1 dbl tr into next dbl tr,
1 dbl tr into next sp, 1 dbl tr into next dbl tr, 2 ch,
6 dbl tr into next sp, remove loop from hook, insert
hook into first tr of tr group and draw thread
through – a popcorn st made, 2 ch) 4 times, 1 dbl tr
into next dbl tr, 1 dbl tr into next sp, 1 dbl tr into

next dbl tr, 5 ch, 1 dc into sp of next shell; repeat
from * omitting 1 dc at end of last repeat, 1 ss into
first dc.
7th Row: 1 dc into same place as ss, 4 ch, * (1 dbl tr
into next dbl tr, 1 ch) 3 times, (1 dbl tr into next sp,
1 ch) twice; repeat from * 3 times more, (1 dbl tr into
next dbl tr, 1 ch) twice, 1 dbl tr into next dbl tr, 4 ch,
1 dc into next dc, 4 ch; repeat from first * omitting
1 dc and 4 ch at end of last repeat, 1 ss into first dc.
8th Row: ** 4 dc into next loop, 1 hlf tr into next dbl
tr, 1 tr into next sp, (1 dbl tr into next dbl tr, 1 dbl tr
into next sp, 1 dbl tr into next dbl tr, 2 ch, a popcorn
st into next sp, 2 ch) 3 times, * (1 dbl tr into next dbl
tr, 1 dbl tr into next sp) twice, 1 dbl tr into next dbl tr,
2 ch, a popcorn st into next sp, 2 ch; repeat from *
twice more, (1 dbl tr into next dbl tr, 1 dbl tr into
next sp, 1 dbl tr into next dbl tr, 2 ch, a popcorn st
into next sp, 2 ch) twice, 1 dbl tr into next dbl tr,
1 dbl tr into next sp, 1 dbl tr into next dbl tr, 1 tr into
next sp, 1 hlf tr into next dbl tr, 4 dc into next loop;
repeat from ** ending with 1 ss into first dc.
9th Row: 1 dc into same place as ss, 1 dc into each of
next 3 sts, * 1 hlf tr into next st, 1 tr into next st, 1 dbl
tr into each of next 2 sts, (1 ch, 1 dbl tr into next sp,
1 ch, 1 dbl tr into next sp, 1 ch, miss 1 st, 1 dbl tr into
next st) 3 times, 1 ch, miss 1 st, 1 dbl tr into next st,
(1 ch, 1 dbl tr into next sp, 1 ch, 1 dbl tr into next sp,
1 ch, miss 1 st, 1 dbl tr into next st, 1 ch, miss 1 st,
1 dbl tr into next st) twice, (1 ch, 1 dbl tr into next sp,
1 ch, 1 dbl tr into next sp, 1 ch, miss 1 st, 1 dbl tr into
next st) 3 times, 1 dbl tr into next st, 1 tr into next st,
1 hlf tr into next st, 1 dc into each of next 8 dc; repeat
from * omitting 4 dc at end of last repeat, 1 ss into
first dc.
10th Row: * 1 dc into next st, (3 ch, miss 1 st, 1 dc
into next st) 33 times, miss 2 sts; repeat from * ending
with 1 ss into first dc. Fasten off.
Damp and pin out to measurements.

To make up
Make a pattern for pin cushion following the crochet
outline. Cut two pieces from fabric by pattern
allowing 1 cm (⅜ in.) for seams. Baste and stitch fabric
on seamline leaving an opening for turning to the
right side. Turn to the right side, stuff with kapok
and oversew open edges together.

Joining crochet sections
1st Row: With wrong sides facing and working
through both sections attach thread to first loop on
last row of second section, 3 dc into same loop, 3 dc
into each of next 65 loops, insert pad and working
through both sections as before work 3 dc into each
loop, 1 ss into first dc.
2nd Row: * 1 dc into each of next 7 dc, 3 ch, miss 5 dc,

(into next dc work 3 tr 3 ch and 3 tr – a shell made –, 1 ch, miss 8 dc) 8 times, a shell into next dc, 3 ch, miss 5 dc, 1 dc into each of next 7 dc, miss 2 dc; repeat from * omitting 7 dc at end of last repeat, 1 ss into first dc. Fasten off.

Scissors Case

Work as pin cushion for 3 rows.

4th Row: 1 ss into each of next 3 sts, 1 dc into same sp, 7 ch, 1 dc into next loop, 12 ch, 1 dc into next loop, 7 ch, 1 dc into sp of next shell, 5 ch, 1 dc into next loop, 7 ch, 1 dc into next loop, 5 ch, a shell into sp of next shell, 5 ch, 1 dc into next loop, 7 ch, 1 dc into next loop, 5 ch, 1 ss into first dc.

5th Row: 1 dc into same place as ss, 7 ch, miss 1 loop, into next loop work (1 dbl tr, 1 ch) 9 times and 1 dbl tr, 7 ch, miss 1 dc, 1 dc into next dc, (5 ch, 1 dc into next loop) 3 times, 5 ch, a shell into sp of next shell, (5 ch, 1 dc into next loop) 3 times, 5 ch, 1 ss into first dc.

6th Row: 1 dc into same place as ss, 7 ch, (1 dbl tr into next dbl tr, 1 dbl tr into next sp, 1 dbl tr into next dbl tr, 2 ch, a popcorn st into next sp, 2 ch) 4 times, 1 dbl tr into next dbl tr, 1 dbl tr into next sp, 1 dbl tr into next dbl tr, 7 ch, 1 dc into next dc, (5 ch, 1 dc into next loop) 4 times, 5 ch, a shell into sp of next shell, (5 ch, 1 dc into next loop) 4 times, 5 ch, 1 ss into first dc.

7th Row: 1 dc into same place as ss, 7 dc into next loop, 1 hlf tr into next dbl tr, 1 tr into next dbl tr, 1 dbl tr into next dbl tr, * (1 ch, 1 dbl tr into next sp) twice, (1 ch, 1 dbl tr into next dbl tr) 3 times; repeat from * twice more, (1 ch, 1 dbl tr into next sp) twice, 1 ch, 1 dbl tr into next dbl tr, 1 tr into next dbl tr, 1 hlf tr into next dbl tr, 7 dc into next loop, (1 dc into next dc, 5 dc into next loop) 5 times, 1 dc into next tr, 3 ch, a shell into sp of next shell, 3 ch, miss 2 tr, 1 dc into next tr, 5 dc into next loop, (1 dc into next dc, 5 dc into next loop) 4 times, 1 ss into first dc.

8th Row: 1 dc into same place as ss, (3 ch, miss 1 st, 1 dc into next st) 43 times, 3 ch, 1 dc into next loop, 3 ch, 1 dc into next tr, 3 ch, a shell into sp of next shell, 3 ch, miss 2 tr, 1 dc into next tr, 3 ch, 1 dc into next loop, 3 ch, 1 dc into next dc, (3 ch, miss 1 st, 1 dc into next st) 14 times, 3 ch, 1 ss into first dc. Fasten off. Make another section in same way. Do not fasten off. Damp and pin out to measurements.
Make a paper pattern for case following the crochet outline.

Joining
1st Row: 3 dc into each of next 28 loops, place sections together wrong sides facing and continue to work through both sections, 3 dc into each of next 18 loops, 1 dc into each of next 3 tr, 3 dc into next loop, 1 dc into each of next 3 tr, 3 dc into each of next 18 loops, 1 ss into first dc.
2nd Row: 1 ss into next dc, 3 ch, into same place as last ss work 2 tr 3 ch and 3 tr, (1 ch, miss 8 dc, a shell into next dc) 9 times, mark last tr of last shell with a coloured thread, (1 ch, miss 8 dc, a shell into next dc) 6 times, (1 ch, miss 5 dc, a shell into next dc) twice, (1 ch, miss 8 dc, a shell into next dc) 5 times, 1 ch, 1 ss into 3rd of 3 ch. Fasten off.

Edging
1st Row: With wrong side facing attach thread to first free loop on first section, 3 dc into same loop, 3 dc into each of next 27 loops, 1 ch, turn.
2nd Row: 1 ss into first dc, 1 ss into next dc, 3 ch, 1 ss into tr marked by thread on second section, into same place as previous ss work 2 tr 3 ch and 3 tr, (1 ch, miss 8 dc, a shell into next dc) 9 times, 1 ss into same place as last ss on 2nd row of joining. Fasten off.

To make up
Cut two pieces from interlining by paper pattern. Cut four pieces from fabric, allowing 1 cm ($\frac{3}{8}$ in.) for seams. Sew edges of interlining together leaving top curved edge open for insertion of scissors. Baste and stitch two fabric sections right sides together leaving curved edge open. Turn to the right side. Repeat with two corresponding fabric sections. Place interlining inside first section. Place remaining section inside this section; turn in top raw edges and slipstitch together. Insert into crochet section and sew round open edge.

Blouse

Coats Chain Mercer-Crochet Cotton No.20 (20 g).
9 (10, 11) balls. This model is worked in shade 503
(Coral Pink), but any other shade of Mercer-Crochet
may be used.
Milward steel crochet hook 1.25 (no.3).

Tension
3 patterns – 5 cm (2 in.) approximately.
First 5 rows – 2.5 cm (1 in.).

Measurements
To fit bust size – 86.5 (91.5, 96.5) cm, 34 (36, 38) in.
Length from centre back – 53.5 (53.5, 59) cm, 21 (21,
22) in., adjustable.

Back
Commence with 218 (234, 250) ch.
1st Row: 1 dc into 2nd ch from hook, * 2 ch, miss 3 ch,
into next ch work 1 tr 3 ch and 1 tr (a V st made), 2 ch,
miss 3 ch, 1 dc into next ch; repeat from * ending
with 1 ch, turn. 27 (29, 31) V sts.
2nd Row: 1 dc into first dc, * into next 2 ch loop work
1 dc 1 hlf tr and 1 tr, 1 tr into next tr, 3 tr into next

3 ch loop, 1 tr into next tr, into next 2 ch loop work
1 tr 1 hlf tr and 1 dc (a shell made over 3 loops and
2 tr); repeat from * ending with 1 dc into next dc, 3 ch,
turn.
3rd Row: Miss first 3 sts, 1 tr into next st, * 4 ch, miss
2 sts, 1 dc into next st, 4 ch, miss 2 sts, leaving the last
loop of each on hook work 1 tr into next st miss 4 sts
and 1 tr into next st, thread over and draw through
all loops on hook (a joint tr made); repeat from *
ending with 4 ch, miss 2 sts, 1 dc into next st, 4 ch,
miss 2 sts, a joint tr working 1 tr into next st miss 2 sts
and 1 tr into next st, 4 ch, turn.
4th Row: 1 tr into first joint tr, * 2 ch, 1 dc into next
dc, 2 ch, a V st into next joint tr; repeat from * ending
with 2 ch, 1 dc into next dc, 2 ch, into next tr work
1 tr 1 ch and 1 tr, 3 ch, turn.
5th Row: 1 tr into first 1 ch sp, 1 tr into next tr, into
next 2 ch loop work 1 tr 1 hlf tr and 1 dc, * a shell over
3 loops and 2 tr; repeat from * ending with into next
2 ch loop work 1 dc 1 hlf tr and 1 tr, 1 tr into next tr,
1 tr into next loop, 1 tr into 3rd of 4 ch, 1 ch, turn.
6th Row: 1 dc into first st, * 4 ch, miss 2 sts, a joint tr
working 1 tr into next tr miss 4 sts and 1 tr into next
tr, 4 ch, miss 2 sts, 1 dc into next st; repeat from *
working last dc into 3rd of 3 ch, 1 ch, turn.

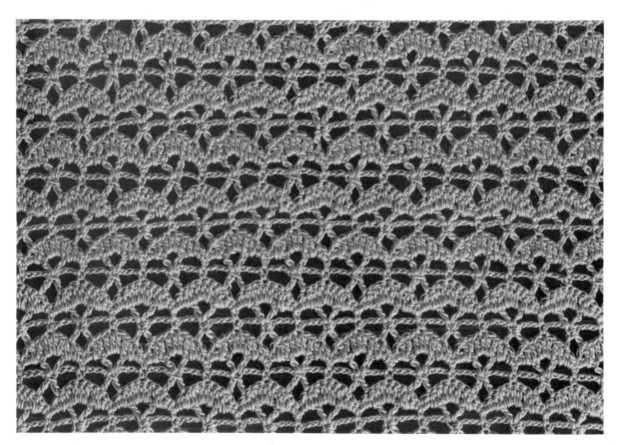

7th Row: 1 dc into first dc, * 2 ch, a V st into next joint tr, 2 ch, 1 dc into next dc; repeat from * to end, 1 ch, turn.
2nd to 7th row forms pattern.
Repeat pattern 11 times more then 2nd to 6th row again or length required ending with a 6th pattern row and omitting turning ch at end of last row.

Armhole shaping
1st Row: 1 ss into each of first 20 sts, 1 dc into next st, work in pattern to within last 20 sts, 1 ch, turn.
2nd Row: As 2nd pattern row omitting turning ch at end of row, turn.
3rd Row: 1 ss into each of first 6 sts, 1 dc into next st, work in pattern to within last 6 sts, 1 ch, turn.
4th Row: As 7th pattern row.
Repeat last 3 rows 3 (3, 4) times.
Continue in pattern for 23 (23, 26) rows more omitting turning ch at end of last row.

Shoulder shaping
1st Row: 1 ss into each of first 10 (10, 5) sts, 1 dc into next dc, work in pattern to within last 10 (10, 5) sts, turn.
2nd Row: 1 ss into each of first 10 sts, 1 dc into next dc, work in pattern to within last 10 sts, turn.
3rd Row: 1 ss into each of first 6 sts, 1 dc into next st, work in pattern to within last 6 sts. Fasten off.

Front
Work as Back until 4th row of Armhole shaping has been completed. Repeat 2nd to 4th row 2 (2, 4) times more then 2nd and 3rd rows again.

Neck shaping (first side)
1st Row: 1 dc into first dc, * 2 ch, a V st into next joint tr, 2 ch, 1 dc into next dc; repeat from * 4 times more, 1 ch, turn.
2nd Row: As 2nd pattern row.
3rd Row: Work in pattern to within last 6 sts, 1 ch, turn.
4th Row: 1 dc into first dc, work in pattern, 3 ch, turn.
5th Row: As 5th pattern row ending with 1 dc into last dc, turn.
6th Row: 1 ss into each of first 6 sts, 1 dc into next st, work in pattern ending with 1 ch, turn.
7th Row: As 7th pattern row.
Repeat 2nd to 7th row once more.
Continue in pattern for 11 rows more omitting turning ch at end of last row, turn.

Shoulder shaping
1st Row: 1 ss into each of first 10 sts, (1 dc into next st, 2 ch, a V st into next joint tr, 2 ch) twice, 1 dc into next dc, 1 ch, turn.
2nd Row: 1 dc into first dc, a shell over 3 loops and 2 tr, 1 dc into next dc, turn.
3rd Row: 1 ss into each of first 6 sts, 1 dc into next st, 4 ch, miss 2 sts, a joint tr working 1 tr into next st miss 2 sts and 1 tr into next st. Fasten off.

Neck and shoulder shaping (second side)
Miss 9 (11, 13) joint tr at centre, attach thread to next dc and complete to correspond with first side.
Sew shoulder and side seams.

Neck edging
1st Row: Attach thread to any shoulder seam, work a row of dc evenly round neck edge having a multiple of 3 dc, 1 ss into first dc.
2nd and **3rd Rows:** 1 dc into each dc, 1 ss into first dc.
4th Row: 1 dc into first dc, * 3 ch, 1 ss into last dc, 1 dc into each of next 3 dc; repeat from * omitting 1 dc at end of last repeat, 1 ss into first dc. Fasten off.

Armhole edgings
Attach thread to underarm seam, work a row of dc evenly round armhole having a multiple of 3 dc and complete to correspond with neck edging.

Lower edging
Attach thread to any side seam, work a row of dc evenly round lower edge having a multiple of 3 dc and complete to correspond with neck edging.
Damp and pin out to measurements.

PINEAPPLE CROCHET

This unique pattern in crochet continues to be ever popular. Its origins are uncertain, but it is said to have been developed from the traditional pine-cone motif found on many Persian and Indian textiles and pot-tery. The crochet interpretation has certainly one of the richest textures of all crochet designs. It is an adaptable style of pattern as can be seen by the following examples.

Pouffe (see plate 6 page 30)

Coats Chain Mercer-Crochet Cotton No.20 (20 g). 20 balls. This model is worked in shade 968 (Dk Orange), but any other shade of Mercer-Crochet may be used.
Milward steel crochet hook 1.25 (no.3).
1.50 m fabric, 122 cm (approximately 48 in.) wide.
Piece of heavy duty foam padding 45.7 × 45.7 × 45.7 cm (18 × 18 × 18 in.).
Coats *Drima* (polyester) thread.

Tension
Size of motif – 15.2 cm (6 in.) square.

Measurements
45.7 × 45.7 × 45.7 cm (18 × 18 × 18 in.).

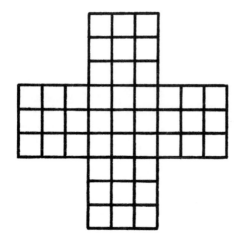

First motif
Commence with 10 ch, join with a ss to form a ring.
1st Row: 4 ch, 4 dbl tr into ring, remove loop from hook, insert hook into 4th of 4 ch and draw drooped loop through (a starting dbl tr popcorn st made), * 3 ch, 5 dbl tr into ring, remove loop from hook, insert hook into first dbl tr of dbl tr group and draw dropped loop through (another dbl tr popcorn st made), 5 ch, a dbl tr popcorn st into ring; repeat from * 3 times more omitting a dbl tr popcorn st at end of last repeat, 1 ss into first popcorn st.
2nd Row: 4 ch, * 3 dbl tr into next sp, 1 dbl tr into next dbl tr popcorn st, into next sp work 3 dbl tr 3 ch and 3 dbl tr, 1 dbl tr into next dbl tr popcorn st; repeat from * omitting 1 dbl tr at end of last repeat, 1 ss into 4th of 4 ch.
3rd Row: 1 ss into next dbl tr, (1 dc into next dbl tr, 5 ch, miss 2 dbl tr) twice, * into next sp work 1 dc 3 ch and 1 dc, (5 ch, miss 2 dbl tr, 1 dc into next dbl tr) 3 times, 5 ch; repeat from * omitting (5 ch, 1 dc) twice and 5 ch at end of last repeat, 2 ch, 1 tr into first dc.
4th Row: 1 dc into loop just formed, (5 ch, 1 dc into next loop) twice, * 11 dbl tr into next loop, (1 dc into next loop, 5 ch) 3 times, 1 dc into next loop; repeat from * omitting (1 dc, 5 ch) twice and 1 dc at end of last repeat, 1 ss into first dc.
5th Row: 1 ss into each of next 3 ch, 3 ch, into same place as ss work 1 tr 3 ch and 2 tr, * 2 ch, 6 tr into centre ch of next loop, remove loop from hook, insert hook into first tr of tr group and draw dropped loop through (a popcorn st made), (1 ch, 1 dbl tr into next dbl tr) 11 times, 1 ch, a popcorn st into centre ch of

next loop, 2 ch, into centre ch of next loop work 2 tr 3 ch and 2 tr (a shell made); repeat from * omitting a shell at end of last repeat, 1 ss into 3rd of 3 ch.

6th Row: 3 ch, * 1 tr into next tr, a shell into next sp, 1 tr into each of next 2 tr, 1 ch, 1 tr into next popcorn st, 1 ch, miss 1 sp, (1 hlf tr into next sp, 1 ch) 10 times, 1 tr into next popcorn st, 1 ch, 1 tr into next tr; repeat from * omitting 1 tr at end of last repeat, 1 ss into 3rd of 3 ch.

7th Row: 3 ch, * 1 tr into each of next 3 tr, a shell into next sp, 1 tr into each of next 4 tr, 2 ch, a popcorn st into next tr, 1 ch, miss 1 sp, (1hlf tr into next sp, 1 ch) 9 times, a popcorn st into next tr, 2 ch, 1 tr into next tr; repeat from * omitting 1 tr at end of last repeat, 1 ss into 3rd of 3 ch.

8th Row: 3 ch, * 1 tr into each of next 5 tr, a shell into next sp, 1 tr into each of next 6 tr, 3 ch, 1 tr into next popcorn st, 1 ch, miss 1 sp, (1 hlf tr into next sp, 1 ch) 8 times, 1 tr into next popcorn st, 3 ch, 1 tr into next tr; repeat from * omitting 1 tr at end of last repeat, 1 ss into 3rd of 3 ch.

9th Row: 3 ch, * 1 tr into each of next 7 tr, a shell into next sp, 1 tr into each of next 8 tr, 4 ch, a popcorn st into next tr, 1 ch, miss 1 sp, (1 hlf tr into next sp, 1 ch) 7 times, a popcorn st into next tr, 4 ch, 1 tr into next tr; repeat from * omitting 1 tr at end of last repeat, 1 ss into 3rd of 3 ch.

10th Row: 3 ch, * 1 tr into each of next 9 tr, a shell into next sp, 1 tr into each of next 10 tr, 5 ch, 1 tr into next popcorn st, 1 ch, miss 1 sp, (1 hlf tr into next sp, 1 ch) 6 times, 1 tr into next popcorn st, 5 ch, 1 tr into next tr; repeat from * omitting 1 tr at end of last repeat, 1 ss into 3rd of 3 ch.

11th Row: 1 dc into same place as ss, * (3 ch, miss 2 tr, 1 dc into next tr) 3 times, 3 ch, a shell into next sp, (3 ch, miss 2 tr, 1 dc into next tr) 4 times, 6 ch, a popcorn st into next tr, 1 ch, miss 1 sp, (1 hlf tr into next sp, 1 ch) 5 times, a popcorn st into next tr, 6 ch, 1 dc into next tr; repeat from * omitting 1 dc at end of last repeat, 1 ss into first dc.

12th Row: 1 ss into next ch, 1 dc into same loop, * (3 ch, 1 dc into next loop) twice, 3 ch, 1 tr into each of next 2 tr, a shell into next sp, 1 tr into each of next 2 tr, 3 ch, miss 1 loop, (1 dc into next loop, 3 ch) twice, 1 dc into next loop, 7 ch, 1 tr into next popcorn st, 1 ch, miss 1 sp, (1 hlf tr into next sp, 1 ch) 4 times, 1 tr into next popcorn st, 7 ch, miss 1 loop, 1 dc into next loop; repeat from * omitting 1 dc at end of last repeat, 1 ss into first dc.

13th Row: 1 ss into next ch, 1 dc into same loop, * 5 ch, 1 dc into next loop, 3 ch, 1 tr into each of next 4 tr, a shell into next sp, 1 tr into each of next 4 tr, 3 ch, miss 1 loop, (1 dc into next loop, 5 ch) twice, 1 dc into next loop, 4 ch, a popcorn st into next tr, 1 ch, miss 1 sp, (1 hlf tr into next sp, 1 ch) 3 times, a popcorn

st into next tr, 4 ch, 1 dc into next loop, 5 ch, 1 dc into next loop; repeat from * omitting 5 ch and 1 dc at end of last repeat, 2 ch, 1 tr into first dc.

14th Row: 1 dc into loop just formed, * 5 ch, 1 dc into next loop, 5 ch, 1 tr into each of next 6 tr, a shell into next sp, 1 tr into each of next 6 tr, 5 ch, miss 1 loop, 1 dc into next loop, 5 ch, 1 dc into next loop, 6 ch, 1 tr into next popcorn st, 1 ch, miss 1 sp, (1 hlf tr into next sp, 1 ch) twice, 1 tr into next popcorn st, 6 ch, miss 1 loop, 1 dc into next loop; repeat from * omitting 1 dc at end of last repeat, 1 ss into first dc.

15th Row: 1 ss into each of next 2 ch, 1 dc into same loop, 6 ch, * 1 tr into each of next 8 tr, a shell into next sp, 1 tr into each of next 8 tr, 6 ch, miss 1 loop, (1 dc into next loop, 6 ch) twice, miss 1 sp, a popcorn st into next sp, 6 ch, miss 1 sp, (1 dc into next loop, 6 ch) twice; repeat from * omitting 6 ch, 1 dc and 6 ch at end of last repeat, 2 ch, 1 dbl tr into first dc.

16th Row: 1 dc into loop just formed, 7 ch, 1 dc into next loop, 7 ch, * 1 dc into each of next 10 tr, into next sp work 2 dc 5 ch and 2 dc, 1 dc into each of next 10 tr, (7 ch, 1 dc into next loop) 6 times, 7 ch; repeat from * omitting (7 ch and 1 dc) twice at end of last repeat, 1 ss into first dc. Fasten off.

Second motif
Work as first motif for 15 rows.

16th Row: 1 dc into loop just formed, 7 ch, 1 dc into next loop, 7 ch, 1 dc into each of next 10 tr, 2 dc into next sp, 2 ch, 1 dc into corresponding loop on first motif, 2 ch, 2 dc into same loop on second motif, 1 dc into each of next 10 tr, (3 ch, 1 dc into next loop on first motif, 3 ch, 1 dc into next loop on second motif) 6 times, 3 ch, 1 dc into next loop on first motif, 3 ch, 1 dc into each of next 10 tr on second motif, 2 dc into next sp, 2 ch, 1 dc into next loop on first motif, 2 ch, 2 dc into same loop on second motif, 1 dc into each of next 10 tr and complete as first motif.

Make 43 more motifs joining each as second motif was joined to first, placing as shown on diagram. Where 4 corners meet join 3rd and 4th motifs to joining of previous motifs.

Damp and pin out to measurements.

To make up
Cutting directions
Sides – Cut two pieces from fabric 94 × 48.5 cm (37 × 19 in.).
Top and Base – Cut two pieces from fabric 48.5 cm (19 in.) square.

Sewing directions
1.5 cm ($\frac{1}{2}$ in.) has been allowed for seams. Place short ends of side sections, right sides together. Baste and stitch. Baste and stitch the top section to the side

section, right sides together, clipping the corners to fit and having the seams at the opposite corners. Turn to the right side. Pull fabric over pad. Place base section in position over pad; turn in seam allowance on side section and sew in position over raw edges of base. Place crochet over pad and sew in position round base and down sides.

Round Motif Cushion (see plate 7 page 31)

Coats Chain Mercer-Crochet Cotton No.20 (20 g).
3 balls. This model is worked in White, but any shade
of Mercer-Crochet may be used.
Milward steel crochet hook 1.25 (no.3).
70 cm fabric, 122 cm (approximately 48 in.) wide.
1.60 m piping cord.
Coats *Drima* (polyester) thread.

Tension
Size of motif – 13.5 cm ($5\frac{1}{4}$ in.) in diameter.

Measurements
51×44.5 cm ($20 \times 17\frac{1}{2}$ in.) approximately.

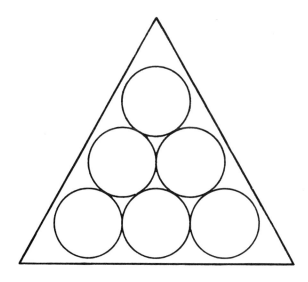

First motif
Commence with 6 ch, join with a ss to form a ring.
1st Row: 9 dc into ring, 1 ss into first dc.
2nd Row: 3 ch, 1 tr into same place as ss, 2 tr into
each dc, 1 ss into 3rd of 3 ch.
3rd Row: 1 dc into same place as ss, * 4 ch, miss 2 tr,
1 dc into next tr; repeat from * ending with 4 ch, 1 ss
into first dc.
4th Row: 1 ss into next loop, 3 ch, 4 tr into same loop,
remove loop from hook, insert hook into 3rd of 3 ch
and draw dropped loop through (a starting popcorn
st made), (3 ch, 5 tr into same loop, remove loop from
hook, insert hook into first tr of tr group and draw
dropped loop through – a popcorn st made) – twice,
* 3 ch, into next loop work (a popcorn st, 3 ch) twice
and a popcorn st; repeat from * ending with 3 ch, 1 ss
into first popcorn st.

5th Row: 1 ss into next loop, 1 dc into same loop,
* 4 ch, 1 dc into next loop; repeat from * ending with
4 ch, 1 ss into first dc.
6th Row: 1 ss into next loop, 3 ch, 6 tr into same loop,
* 1 tr into next loop, 5 ch, 1 tr into next loop, 7 tr into
next loop; repeat from * omitting 7 tr at end of last
repeat, 1 ss into 3rd of 3 ch.
7th Row: 4 ch, * (1 tr into next tr, 1 ch) 5 times, 1 tr
into next tr, 2 ch, into centre ch of next loop work 1 tr
2 ch and 1 tr, 2 ch, miss 1 tr, 1 tr into next tr, 1 ch;
repeat from * omitting 1 tr and 1 ch at end of last
repeat, 1 ss into 3rd of 4 ch.
8th Row: 1 ss into next sp, 3 ch, a starting popcorn st
into same sp, * (2 ch, a popcorn st into next sp)
5 times, 3 ch, miss 1 tr, (1 tr into next tr, 3 ch) twice, a
popcorn st into next 1 ch sp; repeat from * omitting a
popcorn st at end of last repeat, 1 ss into first popcorn
st.
9th Row: 1 ss into next sp, 3 ch, a starting popcorn st
into same sp, * (2 ch, a popcorn st into next sp) 4
times, 3 ch, 1 tr into next tr, 5 ch, 1 tr into next tr,
3 ch, a popcorn st into next 2 ch sp; repeat from *
omitting a popcorn st at end of last repeat, 1 ss into
first popcorn st.
10th Row: 1 ss into next sp, 3 ch, a starting popcorn
st into same sp, * (2 ch, a popcorn st into next sp) 3
times, 3 ch, 1 tr into next tr, 7 tr into next loop, 1 tr
into next tr, 3 ch, a popcorn st into next 2 ch sp;
repeat from * omitting a popcorn st at end of last
repeat, 1 ss into first popcorn st.
11th Row: 1 ss into next sp, 3 ch, a starting popcorn
st into same sp, * (2 ch, a popcorn st into next sp)
twice, 3 ch, (1 tr into next tr, 1 ch) 8 times, 1 tr into
next tr, 3 ch, a popcorn st into next 2 ch sp; repeat
from * omitting a popcorn st at end of last repeat, 1 ss
into first popcorn st.
12th Row: 1 ss into next sp, 3 ch, a starting popcorn st
into same sp, * 2 ch, a popcorn st into next sp, 3 ch,
1 tr into next tr, (5 ch, miss 2 sps, 1 dc into next sp)
twice, 5 ch, miss 2 tr, 1 tr into next tr, 3 ch, a popcorn
st into next 2 ch sp; repeat from * omitting a popcorn
st at end of last repeat, 1 ss into first popcorn st.
13th Row: 1 ss into next sp, 3 ch, a starting popcorn
st into same sp, * 3 ch, 1 tr into next tr, (6 ch, 1 dc into
next loop) 3 times, 6 ch, 1 tr into next tr, 3 ch, a
popcorn st into next 2 ch sp; repeat from * omitting
a popcorn st at end of last repeat, 1 ss into first popcorn st.
14th Row: 1 ss into next sp, 1 dc into same sp, * (6 ch,
1 dc into next loop) 4 times, (6 ch, 1 dc into next sp)
twice; repeat from * omitting 1 dc at end of last repeat,
1 ss into first dc.
15th Row: Into each loop work 3 dc 3 ch and 3 dc, 1 ss
into first dc. Fasten off.

Second motif
Work as first motif for 14 rows.

15th Row: Into next loop work 3 dc 3 ch and 3 dc, 3 dc into next loop, 1 ch, 1 dc into corresponding loop on first motif, 1 ch, (3 dc into same loop on second motif, 3 dc into next loop, 1 ch, 1 dc into next loop on first motif, 1 ch) twice, 3 dc into same loop on second motif and complete as first motif.

Make 4 more motifs joining each as second motif was joined to first leaving 3 loops free between joinings and placing as shown on diagram.

Damp and pin out to measurements.

To make up
Cutting directions
Make a paper pattern to a triangular shape having each side 51 cm (20 in.) long.

Allow 1.5 cm ($\frac{5}{8}$ in.) for seams when cutting out.

Main Sections – Back and Front.

Cut two pieces by pattern.

Gusset – Cut strips 8 cm ($3\frac{1}{4}$ in.) wide by length to fit one main section, joining as necessary to make the required length.

Bias strips for piping cord – Cut strips 5 cm (2 in.) wide to fit cushion, joining as necessary to make the required length.

Sewing directions
Fold bias strip in half lengthwise, wrong sides together, inserting the piping cord. Baste and stitch close to the cord. Baste piping to the right side of one main section, raw edges together, clipping the piping at points of triangle so that it lies flat and joining ends to fit main section. Sew crochet in position. Place gusset to piping, right sides together, joining ends to fit main section. Baste and stitch close to cord. Baste and stitch remaining main section to gusset, leaving an opening for pad insertion. Turn to the right side. Insert pad and slipstitch open edges together.

Coffee Table Mat (see plate 8 page 32)

Coats Chain Mercer-Crochet Cotton No.20 (20 g).
2 balls. This model is worked in shade 789 (Mid Moss Green), but any other shade of Mercer-Crochet may be used.
Milward steel crochet hook 1.25 (no.3).
50 cm fabric, 90 cm (approximately 36 in.) wide.
Coats bias binding to match fabric.

Tension
First 4 rows – 2.5 cm (1 in.).

Measurements
57 cm (22½ in.) in diameter.

First motif
Commence with 4 ch.

1st Row: 1 tr into 4th ch from hook, * 7 ch, 1 quin tr into top of last tr, 3 ch, 1 tr into top of last quin tr, 4 ch, 1 dbl tr into top of last tr, 3 ch, 1 tr into top of last dbl tr; repeat from * twice more omitting 4 ch, 1 dbl tr, 3 ch and 1 tr at end of last repeat.
2nd Row (wrong side): 7 ch, miss first loop, * 9 dbl tr into next loop, 3 ch, 1 dbl tr into next loop, 1 ch, into next loop work 2 tr 2 ch and 2 tr (a shell made), 1 ch, 1 dbl tr into next loop, 3 ch; repeat from * once more, 9 dbl tr into next loop, 3 ch, 1 dbl tr into same place as base of first tr on 1st row, 7 ch, turn.
3rd Row: Miss first dbl tr, * (1 dc into next dbl tr, 9 ch) 8 times, 1 dc into next dbl tr, 3 ch, 1 dbl tr into next dbl tr, 2 ch, a shell into sp of next shell, 2 ch, 1 dbl tr into next dbl tr, 3 ch; repeat from * twice more omitting 2 ch, a shell, 2 ch, 1 dbl tr and 3 ch at end of last repeat and working last dbl tr into 4th of 7 ch, 7 ch, turn.
4th Row: * (1 dc into next 9 ch loop, 3 ch) 8 times, 1 dbl tr into next dbl tr, 2 ch, a shell into sp of next shell, 2 ch, 1 dbl tr into next dbl tr, 3 ch; repeat from * once more ending with (1 dc into next 9 ch loop, 3 ch) 8 times, 1 dbl tr into 4th of 7 ch, 6 ch, turn.

First pineapple
1st Row: Miss first sp, 1 dc into next loop, 3 ch, (into next loop work 1 dc, 3 ch, 1 ss into last dc – a picot made – 3 ch) 5 times, 1 dc into next loop, 3 ch, 1 tr into next dbl tr, 6 ch, turn.
2nd Row: Miss first sp, (1 dc into next loop, 3 ch) 6 times, 1 tr into 3rd of 6 ch, 6 ch, turn.
3rd Row: Miss first sp, 1 dc into next loop, (3 ch, into next loop work 1 dc and a picot) 3 times, 3 ch, 1 dc into next loop, 3 ch, 1 tr into 3rd of 6 ch, 6 ch, turn.
4th Row: Miss first sp, (1 dc into next loop, 3 ch) 4 times, 1 tr into 3rd of 6 ch, 6 ch, turn.
5th Row: Miss first sp, 1 dc into next loop, 3 ch, into

next loop work 1 dc and a picot, 3 ch, 1 dc into next loop, 3 ch, 1 tr into 3rd of 6 ch, 6 ch, turn.
6th Row: Miss first sp, (1 dc into next loop, 3 ch) twice, 1 tr into 3rd of 6 ch, 4 ch, turn.
7th Row: Miss first sp, into next loop work 1 dbl tr 5 ch and 1 dbl tr, 4 ch, 1 ss into 3rd of 6 ch. Fasten off.

Second pineapple
1st Row: With right side facing attach thread to next free dbl tr on 4th row, 6 ch, miss 1 sp, 1 dc into next sp and complete as first pineapple.

Third pineapple
1st Row: With right side facing attach thread to next free dbl tr on 4th row, 6 ch, miss 1 sp, 1 dc into next loop, (3 ch, into next loop work 1 dc and a picot) 5 times, 3 ch, 1 dc into next loop, 3 ch, 1 tr into 4th of 7 ch, 6 ch, turn.
   Complete as first pineapple.

Edging
With right side facing attach thread to row end of 2nd row, 1 dc into same place as join, 5 ch, 1 dc into 4th ch from hook, 1 ch (a picot loop made), (1 dc over next row end, a picot loop) 9 times, * into next sp work 1 dc a picot loop and 1 dc, (a picot loop, 1 dc over next row end) 7 times, 2 ch, into sp of next shell work 3 tr a picot loop and 3 tr, 2 ch, (1 dc over next row end, a picot loop) 7 times; repeat from * once more, into next sp work 1 dc a picot loop and 1 dc, (a picot loop, 1 dc over next row end) 10 times. Fasten off.

Second motif
Work as first motif until 3 pineapples have been completed.

Edging
With right side facing attach thread to row end of 2nd row, 1 dc into same place as join, (a picot loop, 1 dc over next row end) 9 times, a picot loop, 1 dc into next loop, 3 ch, 1 dc into corresponding picot on first motif, 1 ch, 1 dc into 4th st from hook, 1 ch, 1 dc into same loop on second motif, a picot loop and complete as first motif.
   Make 6 more motifs joining each as second motif was joined to first and joining last motif to first motif to correspond.

Heading
1st Row: With right side facing attach thread to picot of 3rd last picot loop made on any motif, 1 dc into same place as join, * (4 ch, 1 dc into next picot) twice, 4 ch, 1 tr into next loop on 1st row of motif, 19 ch, 1 tr into first loop worked on 1st row of motif, (4 ch, 1 dc

into next picot) 3 times, 19 ch, 1 dc into picot of 3rd last picot loop made on next motif; repeat from * omitting 1 dc at end of last repeat, 1 ss into first dc.

2nd Row: 1 dc into same place as join, * (1 dc into each of next 4 ch, 1 dc into next dc) twice, 1 dc into each of next 4 ch, 1 dc into next tr, 1 dc into each of next 19 ch, 1 dc into next tr, (1 dc into each of next 4 ch, 1 dc into next dc) 3 times, 1 dc into each of next 19 ch, 1 dc into next dc; repeat from * omitting 1 dc at end of last repeat, 1 ss into first dc.

3rd Row: 3 ch, into same place as ss work 2 tr 3 ch and 3 tr, * 1 ch, miss 4 dc, 1 dc into next dc, 1 ch, miss 4 dc, into next dc work 3 tr 3 ch and 3 tr; repeat from * omitting 3 tr 3 ch and 3 tr at end of last repeat, 1 ss into 3rd of 3 ch. Fasten off.

Filling
With right side facing attach thread to last loop worked on 1st row of any motif, 3 dc into same loop, 4 dc into next loop, 10 ch, 1 ss into centre ch of 19 ch loop on heading, 10 ch, 1 ss into last dc made, * 3 dc into same loop on motif, (3 dc into next loop, 4 dc into next loop) twice, 12 ch, 1 ss into same place as last ss on heading, 12 ch, 1 ss into last dc made, 3 dc into same loop on motif, (3 dc into next loop, 4 dc into next loop) twice, 10 ch, 1 ss into same place as ss on heading, 10 ch, 1 ss into last dc made, 3 dc into same loop on motif, 3 dc into next loop. Fasten off.

Fill in all sps on motifs in this manner.

Damp and pin out to measurements.

To make up
6 mm ($\frac{1}{4}$ in.) has been allowed for seams.

Cut a circle from fabric 41 cm ($16\frac{1}{4}$ in.) in diameter. Face with bias binding. Sew crochet round edge as in photograph.

Motif Bedspread (see plate 9 page 33)

Coats Chain Mercer-Crochet Cotton No.20 (20 g).
86 balls. This model is worked in White, but any
shade of Mercer-Crochet may be used.
    Milward steel crochet hook 1.25 (no.3).

Tension
Size of motif – 15.2 cm (6 in.) square.

Measurements
198 × 243.5 cm (78 × 96 in.) approximately.

First motif
Commence with 20 ch, join with a ss to form a ring.
1st Row: 36 dc into ring, 1 ss into first dc.
2nd Row: 1 dc into same place as ss, * 8 ch, miss 4 dc,
1 dc into next dc, 7 ch, miss 3 dc, 1 dc into next dc;
repeat from * omitting 1 dc at end of last repeat, 1 ss
into first dc.
3rd Row: 1 ss into next loop, 3 ch, 8 tr into same
loop, * 2 ch, into next loop work 2 tr 2 ch and 2 tr (a
shell made), 2 ch, 9 tr into next loop; repeat from *
omitting 9 tr at end of last repeat, 1 ss into 3rd of 3 ch.
4th Row: 5 ch, * (1 dbl tr into next tr, 1 ch) 7 times,
1 dbl tr into next tr, 3 ch, a shell into sp of next shell,
3 ch, 1 dbl tr into next tr, 1 ch; repeat from * omitting
1 dbl tr and 1 ch at end of last repeat, 1 ss into 4th of
5 ch.
5th Row: * (1 dc into next sp, 3 ch) 7 times, 1 dc into
next sp, 4 ch, into sp of next shell work 2 tr 2 ch 1 tr
2 ch and 2 tr, 4 ch, miss 1 loop; repeat from * ending
with 1 ss into first dc.
6th row: 1 ss into next loop, 3 ch, 5 tr into same loop,
remove loop from hook, insert hook into 3rd of 3 ch
and draw dropped loop through (a starting popcorn
st made), * (3 ch, 6 tr into next loop, remove loop from
hook, insert hook into first tr of tr group and draw
dropped loop through – another popcorn st made)
6 times, 5 ch, (a shell into next 2 ch sp) twice, 5 ch, a
popcorn st into next 3 ch loop; repeat from * omitting
a popcorn st at end of last repeat, 1 ss into first
popcorn st.
7th Row: 1 ss into next loop, 3 ch, a starting popcorn
st into same loop, * (3 ch, a popcorn st into next loop)
5 times, 5 ch, a shell into sp of next shell, 6 ch, a shell
into sp of next shell, 5 ch, a popcorn st into next 3 ch
loop; repeat from * omitting a popcorn st at end of last
repeat, 1 ss into first popcorn st.
8th Row: 1 ss into next loop, 3 ch, a starting popcorn
st into same loop, * (3 ch, a popcorn st into next loop)
4 times, 5 ch, a shell into sp of next shell, 2 ch, 7 tr
into next loop, 2 ch, a shell into sp of next shell, 5 ch,
a popcorn st into next 3 ch loop; repeat from *

omitting a popcorn st at end of last repeat, 1 ss into
first popcorn st.
9th row: 1 ss into next loop, 3 ch, a starting popcorn
st into same loop, * (3 ch, a popcorn st into next loop)
3 times, 5 ch, a shell into sp of next shell, 2 ch, miss
2 tr of shell, (1 tr into next tr, 1 ch) 6 times, 1 tr into
next tr, 2 ch, a shell into sp of next shell, 5 ch, a
popcorn st into next 3 ch loop; repeat from * omitting
a popcorn st at end of last repeat, 1 ss into first
popcorn st.
10th Row: 1 ss into next loop, 3 ch, a starting popcorn st into same loop, * (3 ch, a popcorn st into next
loop) twice, 5 ch, a shell into sp of next shell, 2 ch,
leaving the last loop of each on hook work 3 tr into
next 1 ch sp, thread over and draw through all loops
on hook (a cluster made), (3 ch, a cluster into next sp)
twice, 5 ch, (a cluster into next sp, 3 ch) twice, a
cluster into next sp, 2 ch, a shell into sp of next shell,
5 ch, a popcorn st into next 3 ch loop; repeat from *
omitting a popcorn st at end of last repeat, 1 ss into
first popcorn st.
11th Row: 1 ss into next loop, 3 ch, a starting popcorn st into same loop, * 3 ch, a popcorn st into next
loop, 5 ch, a shell into sp of next shell, 5 ch, a cluster
into next 3 ch loop, 3 ch, a cluster into next sp, 1 ch,
into next loop work 2 tr 3 ch and 2 tr, 1 ch, a cluster
into next loop, 3 ch, a cluster into next loop, 5 ch, a
shell into sp of next shell, 5 ch, a popcorn st into next
3 ch loop; repeat from * omitting a popcorn st at end
of last repeat, 1 ss into first popcorn st.
12th Row: 1 ss into next loop, 3 ch, a starting popcorn st into same loop, * 6 ch, a shell into sp of next
shell, 6 ch, a cluster into next 3 ch loop, 3 ch, 1 tr into
each of next 2 tr, into next sp work 2 tr 3 ch and 2 tr,
1 tr into each of next 2 tr, 3 ch, a cluster into next 3 ch
loop, 6 ch, a shell into sp of next shell, 6 ch, a popcorn
st into next 3 ch loop; repeat from * omitting 6 ch and
a popcorn st at end of last repeat, 3 ch, 1 tr into first
popcorn st.
13th Row: 1 dc into sp just formed, (7 ch, 1 dc into
next sp) 4 times, * 5 ch, into next loop work 2 dbl tr 5
ch and 2 dbl tr, 5 ch, (1 dc into next sp, 7 ch) 7 times,
1 dc into next sp; repeat from * omitting (1 dc, 7 ch)
4 times and 1 dc at end of last repeat, 1 ss into first dc.
Fasten off.

Second motif
Work as first motif for 12 rows.
13th Row: 1 dc into sp just formed, (7 ch, 1 dc into
next sp) 4 times, 5 ch, 2 dbl tr into next loop, 2 ch, 1 dc
into corresponding loop on first motif, 2 ch, 2 dbl tr
into same loop on second motif, 5 ch, 1 dc into next
sp, (3 ch, 1 dc into next 7 ch loop on first motif, 3 ch,
1 dc into next sp on second motif) 7 times, 5 ch, into

next loop work 2 dbl tr 2 ch, 1 dc into corresponding loop on first motif, 2 ch, 2 dbl tr into same loop on second motif, 5 ch and complete as first motif.

Make 13 rows of 16 motifs joining each as second motif was joined to first. Where 4 corners meet join 3rd and 4th motifs to joining of previous motifs.

Damp and pin out to measurements.

IRISH CROCHET

This style of crochet is easily recognizable by the various motifs and background patterns which form the designs.

As has been written earlier, the art of crochet was carried from Europe by the nuns to Ireland and it developed there into quite an individual style.

Irish crochet is different in design from other forms of crochet, as it is worked either with a distinctive mesh background, on which are applied the typical motifs; or else the motif is worked first and then the mesh background is worked round it to form medallions, edgings or all-over lace.

In simple stages, instructions are given for the making of a variety of Irish crochet designs. First there are the background laces, then a selection of motifs. Next, medallions are formed by the linking of single motifs to lace background.

This section is completed by examples of this type of crochet.

Irish Crochet Examples

Chain lace
Make a chain slightly longer than desired length.
1st Row: 1 dc into 10th ch from hook, * 6 ch, miss 3 ch, 1 dc into next ch; repeat from * across, 9 ch, turn.
2nd Row: * 1 dc into next loop, 6 ch; repeat from * across, ending with 6 ch, 1 dc into last loop, 9 ch, turn.

Repeat 2nd row for length required. Fasten off.

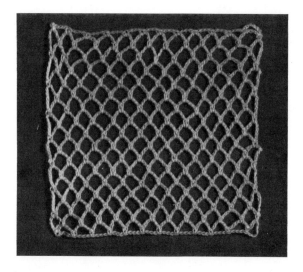

Loop lace

Make a chain slightly longer than desired length.

1st Row: 1 dc into 15th ch from hook, 4 ch, 1 dc into same place, * 10 ch, miss 6 ch, 1 dc 4 ch and 1 dc into next ch; repeat from * across, turn.

2nd Row: Ss to centre of 4 ch loop, 13 ch, * into next 10 ch loop work 1 dc 4 ch and 1 dc, 10 ch; repeat from * across, ending with 1 dc 4 ch and 1 dc into last loop, turn.

Repeat 2nd row for length required. Fasten off.

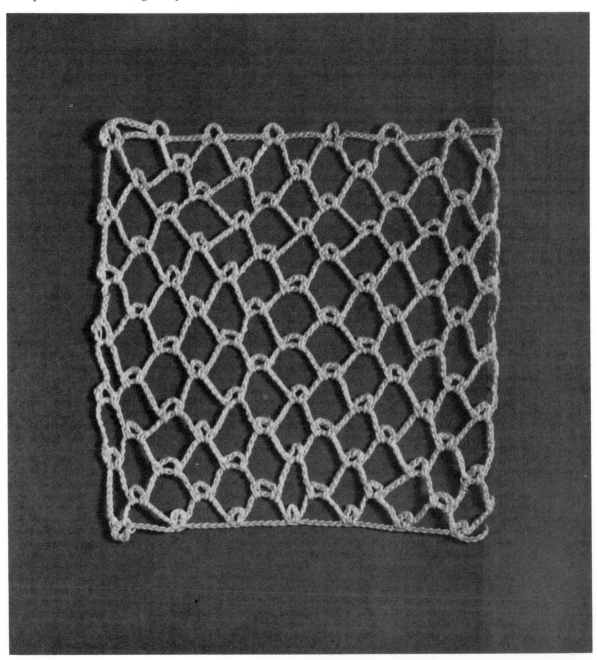

Single picot lace

Make a chain slightly longer than desired length.

1st Row: 1 dc into 3rd ch from hook (picot made), 2 ch, 1 dc into 8th ch from picot, * 6 ch, 1 dc into 3rd ch from hook, 2 ch, miss 4 ch, 1 dc into next ch; repeat from * across, 8 ch, turn.

2nd Row: 1 dc into 3rd ch from hook, 2 ch, 1 dc into first loop (after picot), * 6 ch, 1 dc into 3rd ch from hook, 2 ch, 1 dc into next loop (after picot); repeat from * across, 8 ch, turn.

Repeat 2nd row for length required. Fasten off.

Double picot lace

Make a chain slightly longer than desired length.

1st Row: 1 dc into 3rd ch from hook (picot made), 1 ch, 1 dc into 8th ch from picot, * 3 ch, 1 dc into 3rd ch from hook, 4 ch, 1 dc into 3rd ch from hook, 1 ch, miss 3 ch, 1 dc into next ch (picot loop made); repeat from * across, 7 ch, turn.

2nd Row: 1 dc into 3rd ch from hook, 1 dc between picots of first loop, * 1 picot loop working 1 dc between picots of next loop; repeat from * working last dc into loop after last picot, 7 ch, turn.

Repeat 2nd row for length required. Fasten off.

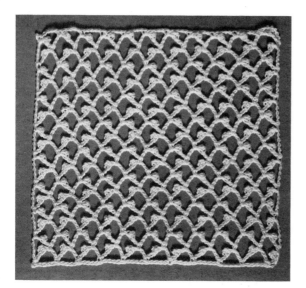

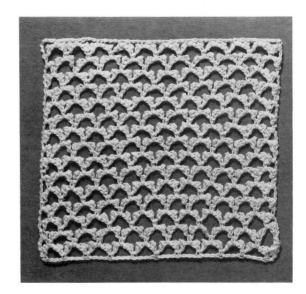

Rose (1)

1st Row: Wind Mercer-Crochet 15 times round end of a pencil, remove from pencil and work 18 dc into ring, join with a ss into first dc.

2nd Row: 1 dc into same place as last ss, * 4 ch, miss 2 dc, 1 dc into next dc; repeat from * 4 times more, 4 ch, miss 2 dc, 1 ss into first dc. (6 loops)

3rd Row: Into each loop work 1 dc 1 hlf tr 3 tr 1 hlf tr and 1 dc, 1 ss into first dc.

4th Row: * 5 ch, 1 dc into next dc on 2nd row inserting hook from behind; repeat from * 4 times more, 5 ch.

5th Row: Into each loop work 1 dc 1 hlf tr 5 tr 1 hlf tr and 1 dc. Fasten off.

Rose (2)

Work same as 1 for 5 rows ending with 1 ss into first dc.

6th Row: * 7 ch, 1 dc into next dc on 4th row inserting hook from behind; repeat from * 4 times more, 7 ch.

7th row: Into each loop work 1 dc 1 hlf tr 6 tr 1 hlf tr and 1 dc, 1 ss into first dc.

8th Row: * 8 ch, 1 dc into next dc on 6th row inserting hook from behind; repeat from * 4 times more, 8 ch.

9th Row: Into each loop work 1 dc 1 hlf tr 7 tr 1 hlf tr and 1 dc, 1 ss into first dc. Fasten off.

Single leaf (1)

Commence with 15 ch.

1st Row: 1 dc into 2nd ch from hook, 1 dc into each ch to within last ch, 3 dc into last ch (tip of leaf), 1 dc into each ch along opposite side of foundation, 1 dc into same place as last dc. Hereafter pick up only the back loop of each dc, 1 dc into each of next 11 dc, 1 ch, turn.

2nd Row: 1 dc into each dc to within centre dc of 3 dc group, into next dc work 1 dc 1 ch and 1 dc, 1 dc into each dc on other side to within 4 dc from centre dc at tip of leaf, 1 ch, turn.

3rd and **4th Rows:** 1 dc into each dc to within 1 ch, into 1 ch sp work 1 dc 1 ch and 1 dc, 1 dc into each dc on other side to within last 3 dc, 1 ch, turn.

5th Row: As 3rd row, making 7 ch instead of 1 ch.

6th Row: 1 dc into each dc to within 7 ch, into 7 ch loop work 2 dc 5 ch 3 dc 5 ch 3 dc 5 ch and 2 dc, 1 dc into each dc on other side of leaf to within last 3 dc. Fasten off.

Triple leaf (2)

Commence with 15 ch, hereafter work over cord (or 4 strands of same thread).

1st Row: 1 dc into 2nd ch from hook, 1 dc into each ch to within last ch, 5 dc into last ch, 1 dc into each ch along opposite side of foundation, 3 dc over cord only. Hereafter pick up only the back loop of each dc, 1 dc into each dc to within 4 dc from centre dc at tip of leaf, 1 ch, turn.

2nd Row: 1 dc into each dc to within centre of 3 dc (over cord), 3 dc into centre dc, 1 dc into each dc on other side to within 4 dc from centre dc at tip of leaf, 1 ch, turn.

3rd Row: 1 dc into each dc to within centre of 3 dc group, 3 dc into centre dc, 1 dc into each dc on other side to within last 3 dc, 1 ch, turn.

4th to 6th Row: As 3rd row, omitting turning ch on last row. Fasten off.

Make 2 more leaves like this.

Sew sides of leaves together to form a triple leaf.

Simple wheel

Commence with 8 ch, join with a ss to form a ring. Work over a cord (or 4 strands of same thread).

1st Row: Into ring work 18 dc.

2nd to 6th Row: 1 dc into each dc increasing 6 dc at equal distances apart (to increase – work 2 dc into 1 dc). Cut off cord, 1 ss into first dc. Fasten off.

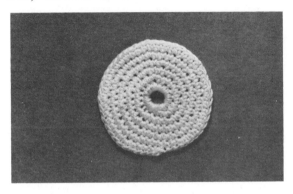

Shamrock

Commence with 10 ch, join with a ss to form a ring, (9 ch, 1 ss into same place as last ss) twice (3 rings made), into first ring work 2 dc 2 hlf tr 12 tr 2 hlf tr and 2 dc, 1 ss into same ch as last ss, (into next ring work 2 dc 2 hlf tr 12 tr 2 hlf tr and 2 dc, 1 ss into same place as last ss) twice, (picking up back loop only work 1 ss into first dc, 1 dc into each of next 18 sts, 1 ss into next dc) 3 times. Fasten off.

Shamrock with shell edging

1st Row: Wind Mercer-Crochet 10 times round end of a pencil, remove from pencil and work 21 dc into ring, 1 ss into back loop of first dc.

2nd Row: 1 dc into same place as last ss, picking up back loop only work 1 dc into each of next 6 dc, * 13 ch, 1 dc into 2nd ch from hook, 1 hlf tr into next ch, 1 tr into each of next 8 ch, 1 hlf tr into next ch, 1 dc into next ch, 1 ss into top of last dc before 13 ch, picking up back loop only work 1 dc into each of next 7 dc; repeat from * twice more, omitting 7 dc at end of last repeat.

3rd Row: * Picking up back loop only work 1 dc into each of next 6 dc, 1 dc into other half of each of 12 ch, 3 dc into turning ch at tip of leaf, 1 dc into each of next 12 sts; repeat from * twice more, 1 ss into back loop of first dc.

4th Row: * Picking up back loop only work 1 dc into each of next 4 dc, 2 ch, miss 1 dc, 1 tr into next dc, (2 ch, miss 2 dc, 1 tr into next dc) 4 times, 2 ch, 3 tr with 2 ch between each into next dc, 2 ch, 1 tr into next dc, (2 ch, miss 2 dc, 1 tr into next dc) 4 times, 2 ch, miss 1 dc; repeat from * twice more, 1 ss into back loop of first dc.

5th Row: * 1 dc into back loop of each of next 2 dc, (5 tr into next sp, 1 dc into next sp) 3 times, 5 tr into next sp, 1 dc into next tr, (5 tr into next sp, 1 dc into next sp) 3 times, 5 tr into next sp, miss 1 dc; repeat from * twice more, omitting 2 dc at end of last repeat, 1 ss into first dc.

Stem

Work 20 dc over cord, 1 ch, turn, picking up back loop only work 1 dc into each dc, 1 ss into dc at base of stem. Fasten off.

Rose Medallion

Commence with 8 ch, join with a ss to form a ring.

1st Row: 6 ch, * 1 tr into ring, 3 ch; repeat from * 4 times more, 1 ss into 3rd of 6 ch. (6 sps made)

2nd Row: Into each sp work 1 dc 1 hlf tr 3 tr 1 hlf tr and 1 dc. (6 petals)

3rd Row: * 5 ch, 1 dc into next tr of 1st row inserting hook from back; repeat from * ending with 5 ch.

4th Row: Into each sp work 1 dc 1 hlf tr 5 tr 1 hlf tr and 1 dc.

5th Row: * 7 ch, 1 dc into next dc on 3rd row inserting hook from back; repeat from * ending with 7 ch.

6th Row: Into each sp work 1 dc 1 hlf tr 7 tr 1 hlf tr and 1 dc.

7th Row: 1 dc into first dc of next petal, * 4 ch, 1 dc into 3rd ch from hook (picot made), 5 ch, 1 dc into 3rd ch from hook (another picot made), 2 ch, 1 dc into centre tr of same petal (a picot loop made), 4 ch, 1 dc into 3rd ch from hook, 5 ch, 1 dc into 3rd ch from hook, 2 ch, 1 dc into first dc of next petal; repeat from * omitting 1 dc at end of last repeat, 1 ss into first dc.

8th Row: Ss to centre of first picot loop (between picots), 1 dc into same loop, * 8 ch, 1 dc between picots of next picot loop, turn, 3 ch, 9 tr into 8 ch loop, 1 tr into next dc, 4 ch, turn, miss first 2 tr, 1 tr into next tr, * 1 ch, miss 1 tr, 1 tr into next tr; repeat from last * twice more, 1 ch, miss 1 tr, 1 tr into top of 3 ch, 4 ch, 1 dc into 3rd ch from hook, 2 ch, 1 dc into same loop as dc after 8 ch, (4 ch, 1 dc into 3rd ch from hook, 5 ch, 1 dc into 3rd ch from hook, 2 ch, 1 dc between picots of next picot loop) twice; repeat from first * omitting 1 dc at end of last repeat, 1 ss into first dc.

9th Row: Ss up side of tr and into each of next 3 ch, 1 dc into sp, * 4 ch, 1 dc into 3rd ch from hook, 5 ch, 1 dc into 3rd ch from hook, 2 ch, miss 1 sp, 1 dc into next sp, 4 ch, 1 dc into 3rd ch from hook, 5 ch, 1 dc into 3rd ch from hook, 2 ch, miss 2 sps, 1 dc into next loop, (4 ch, 1 dc into 3rd ch from hook, 5 ch, 1 dc into 3rd ch from hook, 2 ch, 1 dc between picots of next loop) twice, 4 ch, 1 dc into 3rd ch from hook, 5 ch, 1 dc into 3rd ch from hook, 2 ch, 1 dc into first sp of next block; repeat from * omitting 1 dc at end of last repeat, 1 ss into first dc.

10th Row: Ss to centre of first picot loop, 1 dc into same loop, * 8 ch, 1 dc between picots of next loop, turn, 3 ch, 9 tr into 8 ch loop, 1 tr into next dc, 4 ch, turn, miss 2 tr, 1 tr into next tr, * 1 ch, miss 1 tr, 1 tr into next tr; repeat from last * twice more, 1 ch, miss 1 tr, 1 tr into top of 3 ch, 4 ch, 1 dc into 3rd ch from hook, 2 ch, 1 dc into same loop as dc after 8 ch, (4 ch, 1 dc into 3rd ch from hook, 5 ch, 1 dc into 3rd ch from hook, 2 ch, 1 dc between picots of next loop) 4 times; repeat from first * omitting 1 dc at end of last repeat, 1 ss into first dc.

11th Row: Ss up side of tr and into each of next 3 ch, 1 dc into first sp, * 4 ch, 1 dc into 3rd ch from hook, 5 ch, 1 dc into 3rd ch from hook, 2 ch, miss 1 sp, 1 dc into next sp, 4 ch, 1 dc into 3rd ch from hook, 5 ch, 1 dc into 3rd ch from hook, 2 ch, miss 2 sps, 1 dc into next loop, (4 ch, 1 dc into 3rd ch from hook, 5 ch, 1 dc into 3rd ch from hook, 2 ch, 1 dc between picots of next loop) 4 times, 4 ch, 1 dc into 3rd ch from hook, 5 ch, 1 dc into 3rd ch from hook, 2 ch, 1 dc into first sp of next block; repeat from * omitting 1 dc at end of last repeat, 1 ss into first dc. Fasten off.

Shamrock Medallion

Commence with 2 ch.

1st Row: 6 dc into 2nd ch from hook, 1 ss into first dc.

2nd Row: * 12 ch, miss 1 dc, 1 ss into next dc; repeat from * once more, 12 ch, 1 ss into first dc.

3rd Row: Into each loop work 1 dc 1 hlf tr 15 tr 1 hlf tr and 1 dc, 1 ss into first dc.

4th Row: 1 ss into each of next 2 sts, 1 dc into next st, * (4 ch, 1 dc into 3rd ch from hook, 5 ch, 1 dc into 3rd ch from hook, 2 ch, miss 3 tr, 1 dc into next tr) 3 times, 4 ch, 1 dc into 3rd ch from hook, 5 ch, 1 dc into 3rd ch from hook, 2 ch, 1 dc into 2nd tr of next leaf; repeat from * twice more, omitting 1 dc at end of last repeat, 1 ss into first dc. (12 picot loops)

5th to 8th Row: As 8th to 11th row of Rose Medallion.

Square Mat with Shamrock Edging

Coats Chain Mercer-Crochet Cotton No.20 (20 g).
1 ball White and 1 ball 575 (Mid Laurel Green).
This model is worked in these two shades, but any
other shades of Mercer-Crochet may be used.
  Milward steel crochet hook 1.25 (no.3).

Tension
3 loops – 3 cm ($1\frac{1}{4}$ in.).

Measurements
21 cm ($8\frac{1}{4}$ in.) square.

Single picot mat
Using White, commence with 86 ch.
1st Row: 1 dc into 3rd ch from hook (picot made),
2 ch, 1 dc into 8th ch from picot, * 6 ch, 1 dc into 3rd
ch from hook, 2 ch, miss 4 ch, 1 dc into next ch;
repeat from * 14 times more, 8 ch, turn.
2nd Row: 1 dc into 3rd ch from hook, 2 ch, 1 dc into
first loop (after picot), * 6 ch, 1 dc into 3rd ch from
hook, 2 ch, 1 dc into next loop (after picot); repeat
from * across, 8 ch, turn.
  Repeat 2nd row 28 times more.

Last Row: 1 dc into first loop (after picot), * 4 ch, 1 dc
into next loop (after picot); repeat from * to end of
row. Fasten off.

Shamrock edging
Using Laurel Green, commence with 10 ch, join with
a ss to form a ring, (9 ch, 1 ss into same place as last ss)
twice (3 rings made), into first ring work 2 dc 2 hlf tr
12 tr 2 hlf tr and 2 dc, 1 ss into same ch as last ss, (into
next ring work 2 dc 2 hlf tr 12 tr 2 hlf tr and 2 dc, 1 ss
into same place as last ss) twice, (picking up back loop
only work 1 ss into first dc, 1 dc into each of next
18 sts, 1 ss into next dc) 3 times. Fasten off.

Centre ring
Wind Mercer-Crochet 6 times round end of crochet
hook, remove from hook and work 12 dc into ring,
1 ss into first dc. Fasten off. Sew to centre of shamrock.
  Make 19 more shamrocks in same manner.
  Starch mat and pin out to measurements.
  Sew shamrocks round edge of mat as shown on
diagram.

Cheval Set

Coats Chain Mercer-Crochet Cotton No.40 (20 g).
3 balls White and 1 ball 503 (Coral Pink). This model
is worked in these two shades, but any other shades
of Mercer-Crochet may be used.
Milward steel crochet hook 1.00 (no.4).

Size of Flower – 1.5 cm ($\frac{5}{8}$ in.).

Measurements
Centrepiece – 38 × 24 cm (15 × 9$\frac{3}{8}$ in.).
Small Mat – 16 cm (6$\frac{1}{4}$ in.) square.

Centrepiece
Using White, commence with 151 ch.
1st Row: 1 dc into 3rd ch from hook (picot made),
1 ch, 1 dc into 8th ch from picot, * 3 ch, 1 dc into 3rd
ch from hook, 4 ch, 1 dc into 3rd ch from hook, 1 ch,
miss 3 ch, 1 dc into next ch (picot loop made); repeat
from * across, 7 ch, turn. (36 sps)
2nd Row: 1 dc into 3rd ch from hook, 1 ch, 1 dc
between picots of first loop, * 1 picot loop working
1 dc between picots of next loop; repeat from * 34
times more working last dc into loop after last picot,
7 ch, turn.

Repeat 2nd row 33 times more turning with 5 ch at

end of last row.
36th Row: * 1 dc between picots of next loop, 3 ch;
repeat from * ending with 1 dc into loop after last
picot. Fasten off. (18 turning ch loops on each side.)

Row of flowers

First flower
1st Row: Using White, commence with 6 ch, 1 tr into
6th ch from hook, 2 ch, (1 tr into same place as last tr,
2 ch) twice, 1 ss into 3rd of 5 ch.
2nd Row: Into each 2 ch sp work 1 dc 1 tr 5 dbl tr 1 tr
and 1 dc.
3rd Row: * 5 ch, inserting hook from behind work
1 ss into next tr on first row; repeat from * 3 times
more.
4th Row: Into first loop work 1 dc 1 tr and 4 dbl tr,
remove hook, insert hook into first turning ch loop on
first row and draw loop through, 1 dbl tr 1 tr and 1 dc
into same loop on flower, 1 dc and 1 tr into next loop,
remove hook, insert hook into next sp of foundation
ch and draw loop through, 5 dbl tr 1 tr and 1 dc into
same loop of flower, into each of next 2 loops work
1 dc 1 tr 5 dbl tr 1 tr and 1 dc. Fasten off.

Attach Coral Pink to first dc on 2nd row, 1 dc into
same place as join, 1 dc into each st all round petals,
1 ss into first dc. Fasten off.

Second flower

Work same as first flower for 3 rows.

4th Row: Into first loop work 1 dc 1 tr and 2 dbl tr, remove hook, insert hook into 3rd dbl tr of second last petal worked on 4th row of first flower and draw loop through, 3 dbl tr 1 tr and 1 dc into same loop on second flower, into next loop work 1 dc 1 tr and 2 dbl tr, remove hook, insert hook into 3rd dbl tr of next petal on 4th row of first flower and draw loop through, 2 dbl tr into same loop on second flower, remove hook, insert hook into next sp of foundation ch and draw loop through, 1 dbl tr 1 tr and 1 dc into same loop on second flower, 1 dc and 1 tr into next loop, remove hook, insert hook into next sp of foundation ch and draw loop through, 5 dbl tr 1 tr and 1 dc into same loop on second flower and complete as for first flower.

Make and join 16 more flowers joining as before.

Corner flower

Work same as first flower for 3 rows.

4th Row: Into first loop work 1 dc 1 tr and 2 dbl tr, remove hook, insert hook into 3rd dbl tr of 2nd last petal on previous flower, 3 dbl tr 1 tr and 1 dc into same loop on corner flower, 1 dc 1 tr and 2 dbl tr into next loop, remove hook, insert hook into 3rd dbl tr of next petal on previous flower and complete as for first flower.

Make and join 9 more flowers joining to turning ch loops at side of mat, then work and join another corner flower.

Make and join 18 more flowers joining to chain sps on 36th row, 1 corner flower, 9 more flowers joining to turning ch loops at other side of mat then 4th corner flower joining to corresponding dbl trs on first flower.

Edging

1st Row: Using White, attach thread to 5th dbl tr of any free corner petal, 8 ch, * 1 tr into first dbl tr of next petal, 5 ch, 1 tr into last dbl tr of next petal, 5 ch; repeat from * across, 1 tr into first dbl tr of corner petal, (5 ch, miss 1 dbl tr, 1 tr into next dbl tr) twice, 5 ch; repeat from first * omitting 1 tr and 5 ch at end of last repeat, 1 ss into 3rd of 8 ch.

2nd Row: 5 ch, * 1 tr into 3rd of 5 ch, 2 ch, 1 tr into next tr, 2 ch; repeat from * across, 1 tr into 3rd of 5 ch, 2 ch, into next (corner) tr work 1 tr 6 ch and 1 tr, 2 ch; repeat from first * ending with 1 tr into 3rd of 5 ch, 2 ch, 1 ss into 3rd of 5 ch.

3rd Row: 1 ss into each of next 2 ch, * 1 dc into next tr, (2 dc into next sp, 1 dc into next tr) 4 times, 3 ch, miss 2 sps, 9 tr into next sp, 3 ch, miss 2 sps; repeat from * across, ending with miss 3 sps, into corner sp work 13 tr, 3 ch, miss 3 sps; repeat from first * ending

with 1 ss into first dc.

4th Row: 1 ss into next dc, * 1 dc into each of next 9 dc, 3 ch, 1 tr into each of next 2 tr, (1 ch, 1 tr into next tr) 6 times, 1 tr into next tr, 3 ch, miss 2 dc; repeat from * across, 1 dc into each of next 9 dc, 3 ch, 1 tr into each of next 2 tr, (1 ch, 1 tr into next tr) 10 times, 1 tr into next tr, 3 ch, miss 2 dc; repeat from first * ending with 1 ss into first dc.

5th Row: 1 ss into next dc, * 1 dc into each of next 5 dc, 3 ch, 1 tr into each of next 2 tr, (2 ch, 1 tr into next tr) 6 times, 1 tr into next tr, 3 ch, miss 2 dc; repeat from * across, 1 dc into each of next 5 dc, 3 ch, 1 tr into each of next 2 tr, (2 ch, 1 tr into next tr) 10 times, 1 tr into next tr, 3 ch, miss 2 dc; repeat from first * ending with 1 ss into first dc.

6th Row: 1 ss into next dc, * 1 dc into next dc, 4 ch, 1 tr into each of next 2 tr, (3 ch, 1 tr into next tr) 6 times, 1 tr into next tr, 4 ch, miss 2 dc; repeat from * across, 1 dc into next dc, 4 ch, 1 tr into each of next 2 tr, (3 ch, 1 tr into next tr) 10 times, 1 tr into next tr, 4 ch, miss 2 dc; repeat from first * ending with 1 ss into first dc. Fasten off.

7th Row: Using Coral Pink, attach thread to same place as last ss, 4 ch, * 1 tr into each of next 2 tr, (4 ch, 1 ss into 3rd ch from hook, 2 ch, 1 tr into next tr) 6 times, 1 tr into next tr, 1 dbl tr into next dc; repeat from * across, 1 tr into each of next 2 tr, (4 ch, 1 ss into 3rd ch from hook, 2 ch, 1 tr into next tr) 10 times, 1 tr into next tr, 1 dbl tr into next dc; repeat from first * omitting 1 dbl tr at end of last repeat, 1 ss into 4th of 4 ch. Fasten off.

Small mat (make 2)

Using White, commence with 39 ch.

1st Row: As 1st row of centrepiece having 8 sps instead of 36.

2nd Row: As 2nd row of centrepiece having 6 repeats instead of 34.

Repeat 2nd row 13 times more, turning with 5 ch at end of last row.

16th Row: As 36th row of centrepiece. (8 turning ch loops on each side)

Row of flowers

Make and join 4 flowers along foundation ch same as centrepiece, work 1 corner flower, 4 more flowers joining to turning ch loops at side then work other 2 sides to correspond.

Edging

1st and **2nd Rows:** As 1st and 2nd rows of centre-piece.

3rd Row: 1 dc into same place as last ss; repeat from * to * on 3rd row of centrepiece, ending with miss 2 sps, into corner sp work 13 tr, 3 ch, miss 2 sps; repeat from first * ending with 1 ss into first dc.

4th to 7th Row: As 4th to 7th row of centrepiece.

Damp and pin out to measurements.

FILET CROCHET

Filet crochet is always most popular. It produces a smooth, firm fabric which may be used for a wide variety of articles.

Filet crochet is the simplest type of crochet to work. It consists of a net background made from trebles and chains, the pattern being formed by solid blocks of trebles.

As all filet designs are worked on a pattern of squares, it is easier to follow a diagram than to read written instructions. The first few rows of each design are written, then reference is made to the corresponding diagram which illustrates the remainder of the pattern.

In filet crochet it is extremely important to keep an even and regular tension, as one or two stitches loosely worked can destroy the smooth texture of the crochet.

Cushion (see plate 10 page 34)

Coats Chain Mercer-Crochet Cotton No.40 (20 g). 2 balls. This model is worked in shade 402 (Lt Rose Pink), but any other shade of Mercer-Crochet may be used.

Milward steel crochet hook 1.00 (no.4).
70 cm wine furnishing fabric, 120 cm (approximately 48 in.) wide.
55 cm (22 in.) Lightning zip.

Tension
6 spaces and 6 rows – 2.5 cm (1 in.).

Measurements
38 × 63.5 cm (15 × 25 in.).

Strip (make 2)
Commence with 78 ch.
1st Row: 1 tr into 4th ch from hook, 1 tr into each of next 2 ch, 2 ch, miss 2 ch, 1 tr into next ch (1 sp made), 1 tr into each of next 3 ch (1 blk made), (2 ch, miss 2 ch, 1 tr into next ch) 4 times (4 sps made), 1 tr into each of next 15 ch (5 blks made), 2 ch, miss 2 ch, 1 tr into each of next 16 ch (1 sp and 5 blks made), (2 ch, miss 2 ch, 1 tr into next ch) 4 times (4 sps made), 1 tr into each of next 3 ch (1 blk made), 2 ch, miss 2 ch, 1 tr into each of next 4 ch, 3 ch, turn.

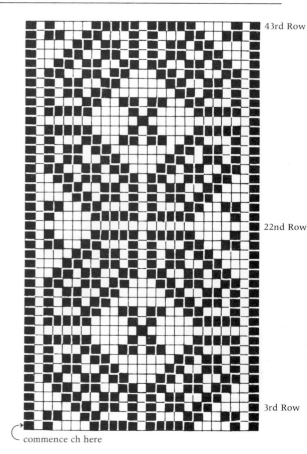

43rd Row

22nd Row

3rd Row

commence ch here

72

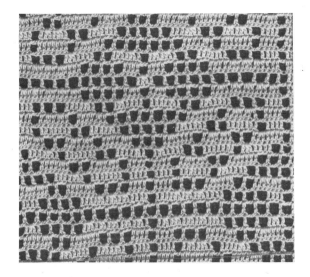

2nd Row: Miss first tr, 1 tr into each of next 3 tr (a blk made over a blk at beginning of row), 2 ch, 1 tr into next tr (1 sp made over 1 sp), 1 tr into each of next 3 tr (1 blk made over 1 blk), 2 tr into next sp, 1 tr into next tr (1 blk made over 1 sp), (2 ch, 1 tr into next tr) twice (2 sps made over 2 sps), 2 blks, (2 ch, miss 2 tr, 1 tr into next tr) 3 times (3 sps made over 3 blks), 1 blk, 1 sp, 1 blk, 3 sps, 2 blks, 2 sps, 2 blks, 1 sp, 1 tr into each of next 3 sts (a blk made at end of row), 3 ch, turn.

Continue to follow diagram from 3rd to 43rd row then from 22nd to 43rd row twice more. Fasten off.

To make up

1.5 cm ($\frac{1}{2}$ in.) seam allowance has been given on all pieces.

Cut 2 pieces 66 × 21.5 cm (26 × 8$\frac{1}{2}$ in.) for back and 1 piece 66 × 40.5 cm (26 × 16 in.) for front of cushion.

Place back sections right sides together, baste and stitch each end of one long side for 5 cm (2 in.). Insert zip to remaining open edges. Place back and front sections right sides together and machine stitch.

Turn to right side.

Sew crochet strips to front 10.5 cm (4$\frac{1}{4}$ in.) from each end.

Filet Bag (see plate 11 page 35)

Coats Chain Mercer-Crochet Cotton No.20 (20 g).
5 balls, or 2 × 50 g balls (see page 7). This model is worked in shade 469 (Geranium), but any other shade of Mercer-Crochet may be used.
Milward steel crochet hook 1.25 (no.3).
1 m fabric, 90 cm (approximately 36 in.) wide for lining.
60 cm Vilene or other bonded fibre interling, 81 cm (approximately 32 in.) wide.
2 rod handles 40.5 cm (16 in.) long.
Coats *Drima* (polyester) thread.

Tension
5 sps and 5 rows – 2.5 cm (1 in.).

Measurements
38.5 × 28 cm (15$\frac{1}{4}$ × 11 in.).

Main Section (make 2)
Commence with 233 ch.
1st Row (right side): 1 tr into 8th ch from hook, (2 ch, miss 2 ch, 1 tr into next ch) 75 times (76 sps made), 5 ch, turn.
2nd Row: Miss first tr, 1 tr into next tr (sp made over sp at beginning of row), (2 ch, miss 2 sts, 1 tr into next tr) 74 times (74 sps made over 74 sps), 2 ch, miss 2 sts, 1 tr into next st (sp made at end of row), 5 ch, turn.
3rd to 9th Row: Follow diagram.
10th Row: 36 sps, (2 tr into next sp, 1 tr into next tr) 3 times (3 blks made over 3 sps), 37 sps, 5 ch, turn.
11th Row: 36 sps, 1 blk, 1 tr into each of next 9 tr (3 blks made over 3 blks), 1 blk, 35 sps, 5 ch, turn.
12th Row: Follow diagram, 5 ch, turn.
13th Row: 26 sps, 5 blks, 4 sps, 3 blks, 2 ch, miss 2 tr, 1 tr into next tr (sp made over blk), follow diagram to end of row, 5 ch, turn.

Continue to follow diagram from 14th to 48th row turning with 5 ch at end of last row.
49th Row: 20 sps, 5 ch, turn.

Continue to follow diagram from 50th row to top. Fasten off. With right side facing miss 36 sps on 48th row, attach thread to next tr, 5 ch, 1 tr into next tr and continue to follow diagram to top. Fasten off.

Gusset
Commence with 50 ch.
1st Row (right side): 1 tr into 8th ch from hook, (2 ch, miss 2 ch, 1 tr into next ch) 14 times (15 sps made), 5 ch, turn.
2nd Row: 15 sps, 5 ch, turn.

Repeat last row 170 times more omitting turning ch at end of last row. Fasten off.

Damp and pin out to measurements.

Joining
Place gusset in position to main section wrong sides together and work a row of dc neatly round 3 sides of gusset and continuing to work over main section only work a row of dc neatly along top edge ending with 1 ss into first dc. Fasten off.

Complete other side to correspond.

To make up
Make a paper pattern for the main section of bag and the bag gusset, following the crochet outline.

Cutting directions
Main section   Cut four pieces by pattern from fabric allowing 1.5 cm ($\frac{1}{2}$ in.) for seams. Cut two pieces by pattern from interlining and trim 3 mm ($\frac{1}{8}$ in.) off all edges.

Gusset   Cut two pieces by pattern from fabric allowing 1.5 cm ($\frac{1}{2}$ in.) for seams. Cut one piece by pattern from interlining and trim 3 mm ($\frac{1}{8}$ in.) off all edges.

Sewing directions
Place an interlining main section centrally to the wrong side of a fabric main section. Baste and stitch close to edge of interlining. Place right side of another fabric section to fabric side of this section, edges even. Baste and stitch on seam line, leaving lower edge open for turning to the right side. Trim seams, clip corners and turn to the right side. Sew open edges together. Make up gusset and other main section in the same way. Insert gusset between main sections and oversew. Insert lining in crochet and sew in position. Fold each handle section in half to the wrong side and sew. Insert handles.

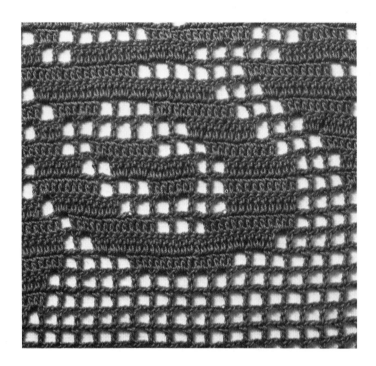

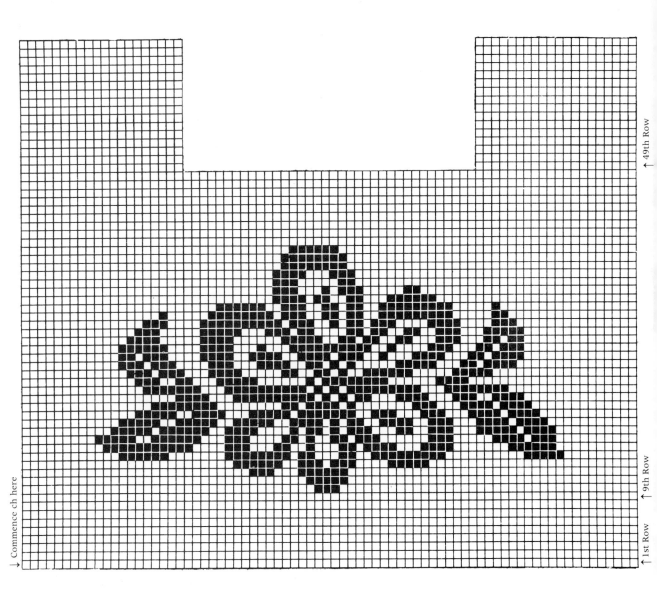

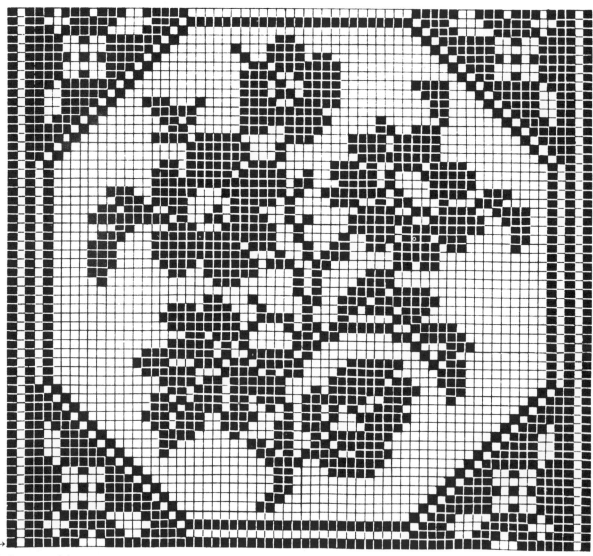

Commence ch here   A

Filet Bedspread (see plate 12 page 36)

Coats Chain Mercer-Crochet Cotton No.20 (20 g).
68 balls.   OR
Coats Chain Mercer-Crochet Cotton No.20 (50 g).
29 balls.
This model is worked in shade 503 (Coral Pink), but
any other shade of Mercer-Crochet may be used.
Milward steel crochet hook 1.25 (no.3).

Tension
5 sps and 5 rows – 2.5 cm (1 in.).

Measurements
243.5 × 149.5 cm (96 × 59 in.).

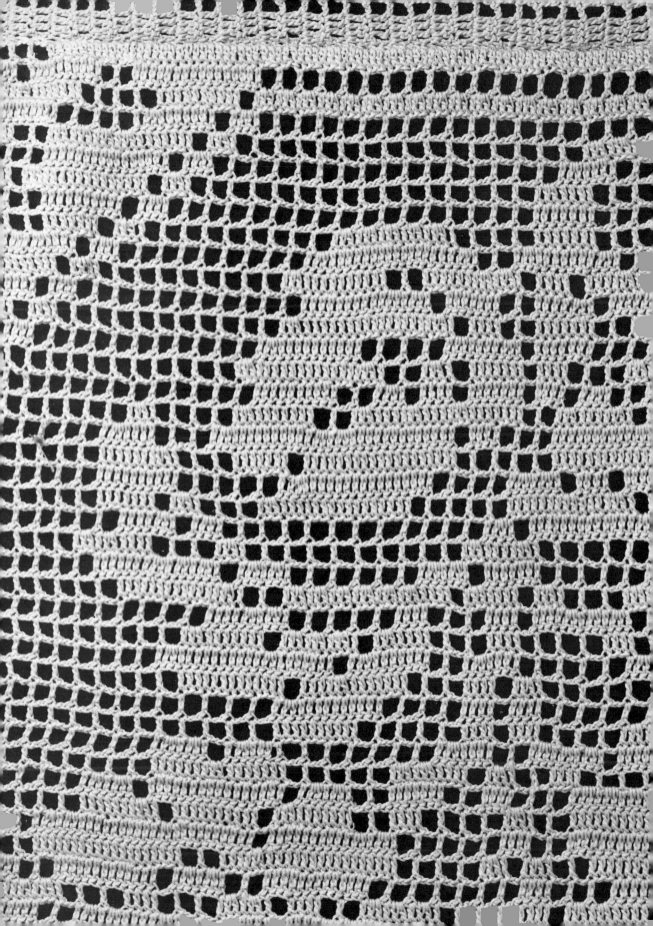

Centre

Strip (make 3)

Commence with 198 ch.

1st Row: 1 tr into 4th ch from hook, 1 tr into each of next 2 ch, 2 ch, miss 2 ch, 1 tr into next ch (a sp made), 1 tr into each of next 18 ch (6 blks made), (2 ch, miss 2 ch, 1 tr into next ch) 3 times (3 sps made), 1 tr into each of next 129 ch (43 blks made), (2 ch, miss 2 ch, 1 tr into next ch) 3 times (3 sps made), 1 tr into each of next 18 ch (6 blks made), 2 ch, miss 2 ch, 1 tr into next ch (a sp made), 1 tr into each of next 3 ch (a blk made), 3 ch, turn.

2nd Row: Miss first tr, 1 tr into each of next 3 tr (a blk made over blk at beginning of row), 2 ch, 1 tr into next tr (a sp made over a sp), 1 tr into each of next 9 tr (3 blks made over 3 blks), 2 ch, miss 2 tr, 1 tr into next tr (a sp made over a blk), 1 tr into each of next 6 tr (2 blks made over 2 blks), 2 tr into next sp, 1 tr into next tr (a blk made over a sp), 1 sp, 3 blks, 2 sps, 5 blks, 25 sps, 5 blks, 2 sps, 3 blks, 1 sp, 3 blks, 1 sp, 3 blks, 1 sp, 1 blk, 3 ch, turn.

3rd to **60th Row:** Follow diagram A.

Repeat 1st to 60th row 7 times more or length required. Fasten off.

Edging

Commence with 117 ch.

1st Row: 1 tr into 4th ch from hook, 1 tr into each of next 2 ch, (2 ch, miss 2 ch, 1 tr into next ch) 5 times (5 sps made), 1 tr into each of next 21 ch (7 blks made), (2 ch, miss 2 ch, 1 tr into next ch) 11 times (11 sps made), 1 tr into each of next 3 ch (a blk made), 2 ch, miss 2 ch, 1 tr into next ch (a sp made), 1 blk, 4 sps, 1 blk, 1 sp, 1 blk, 2 sps, 2 blks, 8 ch, turn.

2nd Row: 1 tr into 4th ch from hook, 1 tr into each of next 4 ch (2 blks increased at beginning of row), 1 tr into each of next 4 tr (a blk made over a blk), 2 ch, miss 2 tr, 1 tr into next tr (a sp made over a blk), (2 ch, 1 tr into next tr) twice (2 sps made over 2 sps), 1 sp, 2 tr into next sp, 1 tr into next tr (a blk made over a sp), 6 sps, 2 blks, 9 sps, 2 blks, 2 sps, 1 blk, 1 sp, 1 blk, 2 sps, 2 blks, 3 sps, 1 blk, 3 ch, turn.

3rd to **48th Row:** Follow diagram B.

Repeat 1st to 48th row 23 times more then 1st to 25th row again or length required. Fasten off.

Damp and pin out to measurements.

To make up

Sew strips for centre neatly together, then sew edging in position round three sides gathering slightly at each corner.

Damp and press.

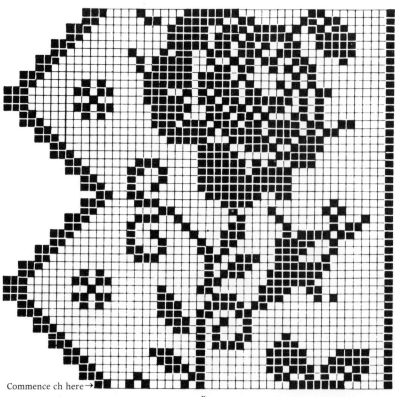

Commence ch here→

B

HAIRPIN LACE CROCHET

This particularly charming type of crochet has a wide variety of uses; as an edging for collar, handkerchief, tray mat and guest towel or as an all-over pattern for cushion, lampshade or coffee table mat.

Hairpin crochet is very easy to work and uses a comparatively small amount of yarn as long loops form the longest part of the fabric.

Edging for Handkerchief (see plate 13 page 37)

Coats Chain Mercer-Crochet Cotton No.40 (20 g).
1 ball. This model is worked in shade 795 (Amber Gold), but any other shade of Mercer-Crochet may be used.
  Milward steel crochet hook 1.00 (no.4).
  Hairpin lace staple 2.5 cm (1 in.) wide.
  1 handkerchief.
  Depth of edging – 3.4 cm (1⅜ in.).
  How to work the lace – see page 17.
  Work a piece of hairpin lace for length required without stretching plus 2.5 cm (1 in.) for each corner having a multiple of 6 loops for each side and 13 loops for each corner. Join at centre. Fasten off. Keep loops twisted throughout.

Heading
Attach thread to first 6 loops, 1 dc into same place as join, * 8 ch, 1 dc into next 6 loops (a cluster made); repeat from * along side, 8 ch, 1 dc into next 13 loops (corner); repeat from first * 3 times more ending with 8 ch, 1 ss into first dc. Fasten off.

Edging
1st Row: With right side facing miss first 3 loops on opposite side of hairpin lace, attach thread to next 3 loops, 4 ch, into same place as join work (1 tr, 1 ch) 5 times, ** into next loop work (1 tr, 1 ch) 6 times, into next 3 loops work (1 tr, 1 ch) 6 times (corner turned), * into next 6 loops work (1 tr, 1 ch) 6 times; repeat from * along side ending with into next 3 loops work (1 tr, 1 ch) 6 times; repeat from ** omitting (1 tr,

1 ch) 6 times at end of last repeat, 1 ss into 3rd of 4 ch.
2nd Row: * (1 dc into next sp, 3 ch) 4 times, (1 dc into next sp) twice; repeat from * ending with 1 ss into first dc.
3rd Row: 1 ss into next ch, 1 dc into same sp, (3 ch, 1 dc into next sp) 3 times, * 3 ch, miss 1 dc, 1 dc into next dc, (3 ch, 1 dc into next sp) 4 times; repeat from * ending with 3 ch, miss 1 dc, 1 dc into next dc, 3 ch, 1 ss into first dc. Fasten off.

  Damp and pin out to measurements.
  Sew edging to handkerchief.

79

Hairpin Lace Cushion

Coats Chain Mercer-Crochet No.10 (20 g).
7 balls. This model is worked in shade 403 (Rose Pink), but any other shade of Mercer-Crochet may be used.
    Milward steel crochet hook 1.50 (no.2½).
    Hairpin lace staple 3.2 cm (1¼ in.) wide.
Cushion pad in contrasting colour 40.5 cm (16 in.) in diameter.

Measurement
43 cm (17 in.) in diameter.

Side (make 2)
First strip   Work a piece of hairpin lace having 36 loops on each side. Join at centre. Fasten off.
    Keep loops twisted throughout.

Centre   Attach thread to first 6 loops, 1 dc into same place as join, (2 ch, 1 dc into next 6 loops) 5 times, 2 ch, 1 ss into first dc. Fasten off.

Edging
1st Row: With right side facing attach thread to first loop on opposite side of centre strip, 1 dc into same place as join, * 2 ch, 1 dc into next loop; repeat from * ending with 2 ch, 1 ss into first dc.
2nd Row: Into same place as ss work 1 dc 3 ch and 1 dc (a picot made), * 2 dc into next sp, a picot into next dc; repeat from * ending with 2 dc into next sp, 1 ss into first dc.
3rd Row: 1 dc into first picot, * into next picot work 3 tr 3 ch and 3 tr (a shell made), 1 dc into next picot; repeat from * omitting 1 dc at end of last repeat, 1 ss into first dc. Fasten off.

Second strip   Work a piece of hairpin lace having 108 loops on each side. Join at centre. Fasten off.

Joining   **1st Row:** Attach thread to first 6 loops, 1 dc into same place as join, * 7 ch, 1 dc into next 6 loops; repeat from * ending with 7 ch, 1 ss into first dc.
2nd Row: A picot into same place as ss, * into next loop work 4 dc 3 ch and 4 dc, a picot into next dc; repeat from * omitting a picot at end of last repeat, 1 ss into first dc.
3rd Row: 1 dc into first picot, into next loop work 1 dbl tr 2 tr 1 ch 1 dc into 3 ch sp of any shell on first strip 1 ch 2 tr and 1 dbl tr, * 1 dc into next picot, into

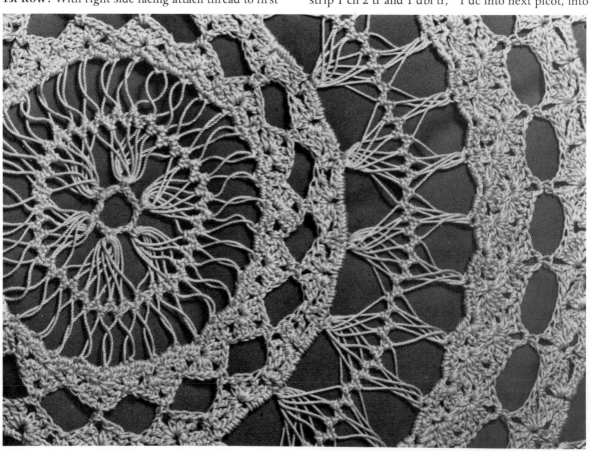

80

next loop work 1 dbl tr 2 tr 1 ch 1 dc into next shell on first strip 1 ch 2 tr and 1 dbl tr; repeat from * ending with 1 ss into first dc. Fasten off.

Edging

1st Row: With right side facing attach thread to first 3 loops on opposite side of strip, 1 dc into same place as join, * 7 ch, 1 dc into next 3 loops; repeat from * ending with 7 ch, 1 ss into first dc.

2nd Row: A picot into same place as ss, * into next sp work 3 dc 3 ch and 3 dc, a picot into next dc; repeat from * omitting a picot at end of last repeat, 1 ss into first dc.

3rd Row: 1 dc into first picot, * a shell into next loop, 1 dc into next picot; repeat from * ending with a shell into next loop, 1 ss into first dc.

4th Row: 3 ch, into same place as ss work 2 tr 3 ch and 3 tr, * 1 dc into next sp, a shell into next dc; repeat from * ending with 1 dc into next sp, 1 ss into 3rd of 3 ch.

5th Row: 1 ss into each of next 2 sts, * 1 dc into next sp, into next dc work 1 dbl tr 2 tr 3 ch 2 tr and 1 dbl tr; repeat from * ending with 1 ss into first dc. Fasten off.

Third strip Work a piece of hairpin lace having 288 loops on each side. Join at centre. Fasten off.

Joining **1st Row:** Attach thread to first 8 loops, 1 dc into same place as join, * 9 ch, 1 dc into next 8 loops; repeat from * ending with 9 ch, 1 ss into first dc.

2nd Row: A picot into same place as ss, * into next sp work 5 dc 3 ch and 5 dc, a picot into next dc; repeat from * omitting a picot at end of last repeat, 1 ss into first dc.

3rd Row: 1 dc into first picot, * into next loop work 1 trip tr 1 dbl tr 1 tr 3 ch 1 tr 1 dbl tr and 1 trip tr, 1 dc into next picot; repeat from * omitting 1 dc at end of last repeat, 1 ss into first dc.

4th Row: 4 ch, 2 tr into same place as ss, 1 ch, 1 dc into sp of any shell on 5th row of Edging on second strip, 1 ch, into same place as last tr on third strip work 2 tr and 1 dbl tr, * 1 dc into next sp, into next dc work 1 dbl tr 2 tr 1 ch, 1 dc into sp of next shell on second strip, 1 ch, into same place as last tr on third strip work 2 tr and 1 dbl tr; repeat from * ending with 1 dc into next sp, 1 ss into 4th of 4 ch. Fasten off.

Edging **1st Row:** With right side facing miss first 2 loops on opposite side of third strip, attach thread to next 4 loops, 1 dc into same place as join, * 5 ch, 1 dc into next 4 loops; repeat from * ending with 5 ch, 1 ss into first dc.

2nd Row: A picot into same place as ss, * into next sp work 3 dc 3 ch and 3 dc, a picot into next dc; repeat from * omitting a picot at end of last repeat, 1 ss into

first dc.

3rd Row: * 1 dc into next picot, a shell into next loop; repeat from * ending with 1 ss into first dc.

4th Row: 3 ch, into same place as ss work 2 tr 3 ch and 3 tr, * 1 dc into next sp, a shell into next dc; repeat from * ending with 1 dc into next sp, 1 ss into 3rd of 3 ch.

5th Row: 1 ss into each of next 2 sts, * 1 dc into next sp, a shell into next dc; repeat from * ending with 1 ss into first dc.

Repeat last 2 rows once more. Fasten off.

Damp and pin out to measurements.

Joining **1st Row:** Place wrong side of sections together matching pattern, attach thread to any sp and working over both sections 3 dc into same place as join, (5 ch, 3 dc into next sp) 57 times, continue in this manner working over one section only ending with 5 ch, 1 ss into first dc.

2nd Row: 1 ss into next dc, 3 ch, into same place as ss work 2 tr 3 ch and 3 tr, * 1 dc into next loop, miss 1 dc, a shell into next dc; repeat from * ending with 1 dc into next loop, 1 ss into 3rd of 3 ch. Fasten off.

Insert pad and slipstitch opening.

Hairpin Lace Stole (see plate 14 page 38)

Coats Chain Mercer-Crochet Cotton No.20 (20 g).
9 balls. This model is worked in Black, but any shade
of Mercer-Crochet may be used.
  Milward steel crochet hook 1.25 (no.3).
  Hairpin lace staple 4.5 cm (1¾ in.).

Tension
Depth of one strip – 8.5 cm (3⅜ in.).

Measurements
41 × 152 cm (16¼ × 60 in.).

  How to Work the Lace (see page 17 for steps 1
to 7).
  Step 8: 1 dc into same loop of left prong.
  Repeat steps 1 to 8 for length required.

First strip
Make a piece of hairpin lace having 402 loops on each
side or length required having a multiple of 20 loops
plus 2 on each side. Fasten off. Keep loops twisted
throughout.

First side
1st Row: Attach thread to first 6 loops, 1 dc into same
place as join, * (7 ch, 1 dc into next 2 loops) 5 times,
7 ch, 1 dc into next 10 loops; repeat from * working
last dc into remaining 6 loops, 3 ch, turn.
2nd Row (right side): (7 tr into next loop, 1 tr into
next dc) 5 times, * 3 tr into next loop, leaving the last
loop of each on hook work 1 tr into same loop and
1 tr into next loop, thread over and draw through all
loops on hook (a joint tr made), 3 tr into same loop,
(1 tr into next dc, 7 tr into next loop) 4 times, 1 tr into
next dc; repeat from * ending with 7 tr into next loop,
1 tr into next dc, 7 ch, turn.
3rd Row: Miss first 8 tr, * (1 dc into next tr, 5 ch, miss
3 tr) 4 times, into next tr work 1 tr 5 ch and 1 tr (a V
st made), (5 ch, miss 3 tr, 1 dc into next tr) 4 times,
7 ch, miss 7 sts; repeat from * omitting 7 ch at end of
last repeat, 3 ch, miss 7 tr, 1 dbl tr into next st.
Fasten off.

Second side

1st Row: With wrong side facing attach thread to first 2 loops on opposite side of strip, 1 dc into same place as join, (7 ch, 1 dc into next 2 loops) twice, * 7 ch, 1 dc into next 10 loops, (7 ch, 1 dc into next 2 loops) 5 times; repeat from * omitting (7 ch, 1 dc) twice at end of last repeat, 3 ch, turn.

2nd Row: (7 tr into next loop, 1 tr into next dc) twice, * 3 tr into next loop, a joint tr into same loop and into next loop, 3 tr into same loop, (1 tr into next dc, 7 tr into next loop) 4 times, 1 tr into next dc; repeat from * omitting 16 tr at end of last repeat, 8 ch, turn.

3rd Row: 1 tr into first tr, * (5 ch, miss 3 tr, 1 dc into next tr) 4 times, 7 ch, miss 7 sts, 1 dc into next tr, (5 ch, miss 3 tr, 1 dc into next tr) 3 times, 5 ch, miss 3 tr, a V st into next tr; repeat from * working last V st into top of turning ch. Fasten off.

Second strip

Work as first strip.

First side

Work as first side of first strip.

Second side

Work as second side of first strip for 2nd row turning with 5 ch instead of 8 ch.

3rd Row: 1 dc into dbl tr on 3rd row of first side on first strip, 2 ch, 1 tr into first tr on second strip, * (2 ch, 1 dc into next loop on first strip, 2 ch, miss 3 tr on second strip, 1 dc into next tr) 4 times, 3 ch, 1 dc into next V st on first strip, 3 ch, miss 7 sts on second strip, 1 dc into next tr, (2 ch, 1 dc into next loop on first strip, 2 ch, miss 3 tr on second strip, 1 dc into next tr) 3 times, 2 ch, 1 dc into next loop on first strip, 2 ch, miss 3 tr on second strip, 1 tr into next st, 2 ch, 1 dc into next loop on first strip, 2 ch, 1 tr into same place as last tr on second strip; repeat from * omitting 1 dc 2 ch and 1 tr at end of last repeat, 1 dc into 4th ch of next loop on first strip, 2 ch, 1 tr into same place as last tr on second strip. Fasten off.

Make 3 more strips joining each as second strip was joined to first.

Edging

1st Row: With wrong side facing attach thread to top of last dbl tr on first side of last strip and continue to work over row ends, 4 ch, 1 dc over next tr row end, * 9 ch, into centre of hairpin strip work 1 tr, 4 ch and 1 tr, 9 ch, 1 dc over next tr row end, (4 ch, 1 dc over next row end) 3 times; repeat from * omitting (1 dc, 4 ch) twice and 1 dc at end of last repeat, 1 dc into 3rd of 8 turning ch, 3 ch, turn.

2nd Row: 4 tr into first loop, 1 tr into next dc, * 9 tr into next loop, 1 tr into next tr, 4 tr into next loop, 1 tr

into next tr, 9 tr into next loop, (1 tr into next dc, 4 tr into next loop) 3 times, 1 tr into next dc; repeat from * omitting 10 tr at end of last repeat, 1 ch, turn.

3rd Row: 1 dc into first tr, * 5 ch, miss 4 tr, 1 dc into next st; repeat from * to end. Fasten off.

Work other side to correspond.

Damp and pin out to measurements.

Fringe

Cut sufficient groups of 12 strands 41 cm (16 in.) long. Place one group in each loop on edging along each end of stole as shown in illustration.

TATTING

The art of tatting seems to have originated on the Continent, where an early form of it was very popular in the eighteenth century.

It was the Victorians who first revived the art and considerably improved the process of working.

After the First World War, along with the general neglect of all things Victorian, it fell out of use.

A few years ago, along with other handicrafts, it was widely revived. The possibilities of tatting for present-day fashion were first seen in France, and have since been followed up with great success in Britain and America. This fascinating craft is now being used to glamorize clothes as well as household linens of all kinds.

Tatting has become for the third time in two hundred years a modish pastime, and it looks likely to be an enduring vogue.

Tatting has intricate beauty but is simple to learn. In the following pages, full and clear instructions are given on tatting, followed by a few designs.

How to tat

1 Hold the flat side of the shuttle in a horizontal position, between the thumb and the forefinger of the right hand. Allow approximately 38 cm (15 in.) of the shuttle thread to hang free from the back of the shuttle.

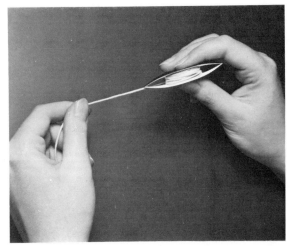

2 Grasp the free end of the shuttle thread between the thumb and the forefinger of the left hand.

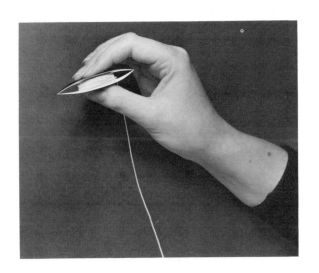

3 Spread out the middle, ring and little fingers of the left hand and pass the thread over them.

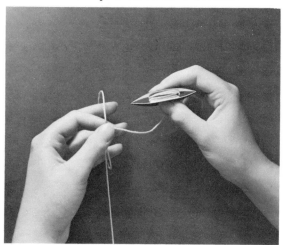

4 Bring the thread round the fingers of the left hand to form a circle and hold it securely between the thumb and the forefinger.

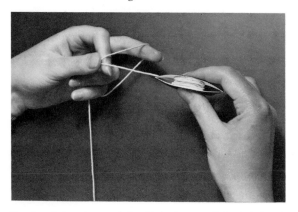

5 Bend the ring and the little finger of the left hand to catch the thread against the palm.

6 Raise the middle finger of the left hand to 'open' the circle.

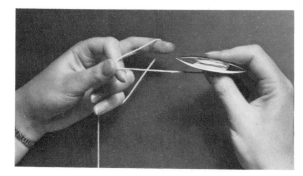

7 Adjust the thread so that the fingers do not feel strained and draw the shuttle thread out to its full length keeping the right and left hands at equal levels.

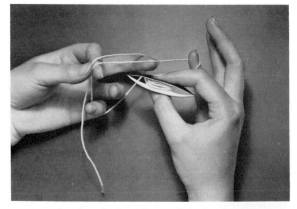

8 Pass the shuttle thread round the back of the little finger of the right hand. Both hands are now in position to commence the basic stitch in tatting known as the Double Stitch.

First half of double stitch

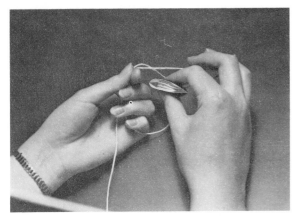

9 With the thread in position, drop the middle finger of the left hand and move the shuttle forward passing it under the shuttle thread and through the circle.

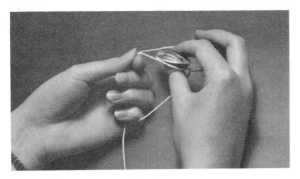

10 Bring the shuttle back over the circle of thread and under the shuttle thread.

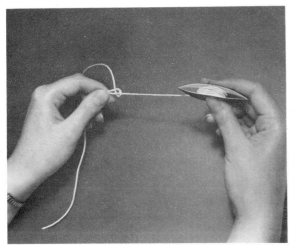

11 Drop the thread from the little finger of the right hand and draw the shuttle thread taut with a sharp jerk.

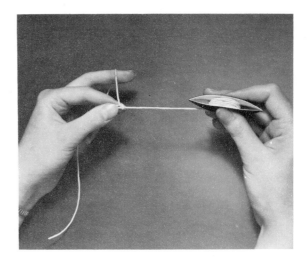

12 Slowly raise the middle finger of the left hand, slide the loop into position between the thumb and forefinger. This completes the first half of the double stitch.

Second half of double stitch

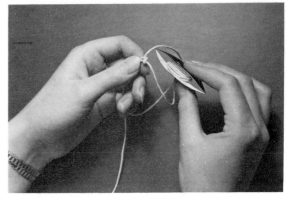

13 and 14 Move the shuttle forward, dropping the shuttle thread and passing the shuttle over the circle and back through between the circle and shuttle threads.

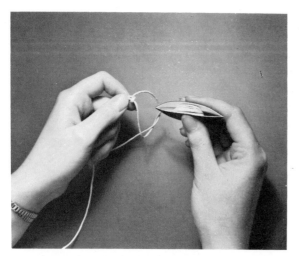

15 Drop the middle finger of the left hand.

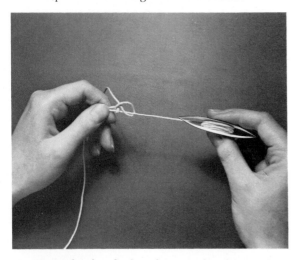

16 Draw the shuttle thread taut with a sharp jerk.

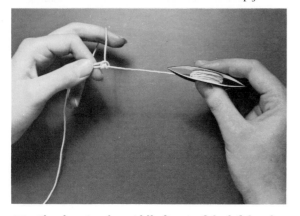

17 Slowly raise the middle finger of the left hand to slide the loop into position next to the first half of the stitch. This completes the second half of the double stitch.

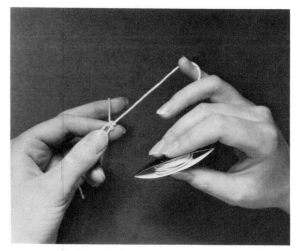

18 This shows hands and shuttle in position to commence next double stitch.

Once this stitch has been properly mastered you should be able to work any of the designs in this book.

Practise the following directions. They give in detail the fundamentals of rings, picots and joinings.

· Rings, picots and joinings

First ring
As each double stitch is formed slide it along the circle of thread to meet the preceding double stitch. Hold them securely between the thumb and forefinger. (See the arrows in figures 19, 20 and 21.)

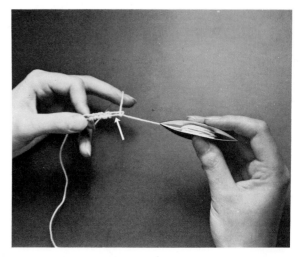

19 Make four double stitches. Then make the first half of a double stitch sliding it to within 6 mm ($\frac{1}{4}$ in.) of the preceding stitch.

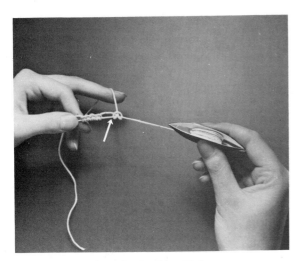

20 Now complete the double stitch.

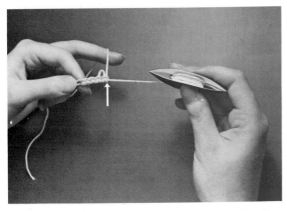

21 Slide the stitch along the ring to meet the first four double stitches. The small loop formed between the last two double stitches is a picot. The size of this may be altered as desired by adjusting the space left from the preceding stitch. Make three more double stitches. Make a second picot and four double stitches. Make a third picot and four double stitches.

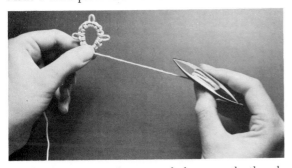

22 Holding the stitches securely between the thumb and forefinger of the left hand, draw the shuttle thread tight so that the first and last stitches meet forming a ring.

In general instructions the ring just completed would be written as: R of 4 ds, 3 ps sep by 4 ds, 4 ds, cl.

Second ring and joining

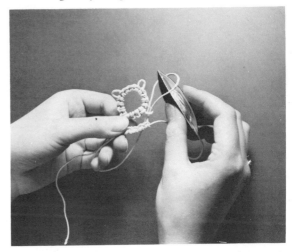

23 (i) Wind the thread round the left hand in position for another ring. Leaving a space of 6 mm ($\frac{1}{4}$ in.) from base of previous ring, make *four* double stitches. (ii) Insert the hook through the last picot of the previous ring and pull the circle thread through, being careful not to twist it as you do so. (iii) Pass the shuttle through the loop. Slowly raise the middle finger of the left hand to draw up the loop. This stands as the first half of the next double stitch. (iv) Now work the second half of a double stitch. (A joining and one double stitch have now been completed.) Work 3 ds, 2 ps sep by 4 ds, 4 ds, cl. (second ring completed).

Using ball thread and shuttle

The preceding instructions have been given in detail so that you may easily understand the various stages and their abbreviations. Now you are ready to read the same instructions as they will appear later in the book. When your rings are even and your picots uniform in size, proficiency should be acquired in the use of the ball thread and shuttle thread before attempting to follow a full set of instructions. The ball thread is used only in the working of chains. Rings are made with the shuttle thread.

Although some designs are made up of rings and others only contain chains, most designs consist of a combination of these two. For these it is necessary to use the shuttle thread and the ball thread. Commence by tying the ends of the two threads together. Make a ring as before.

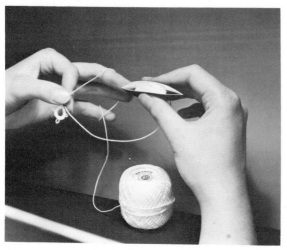

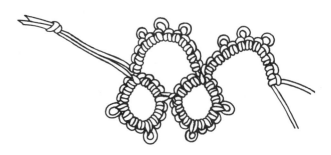

24   Unlike rings, chains are made with the thread held across the back of the fingers of the left hand, winding it round the little finger to control the tension.

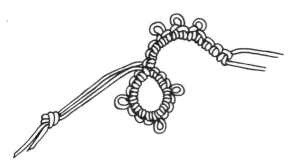

25   A chain consists of a given number of double stitches worked over the ball thread with the shuttle.
    A chain may also include picots.

Reversing

26   In tatting it will be noticed that the rounded end of the working ring or chain faces upwards. When working a design of rings and chains it is sometimes necessary to reverse work. (See also figure 27.)

27   To reverse work turn the ring or chain just completed to face downwards, ie in the reverse position. The next ring or chain is then worked in the usual way having the rounded end facing upwards.

Two shuttles

When rings are to be worked in two colours, two shuttles are used. The two colours (one in each shuttle) may be alternated. When this takes place the shuttle which made the preceding ring is dropped, the second shuttle is picked up and a ring is made as before. When the rings are separated by a chain, the thread of the second shuttle is held similarly to the ball thread in figure 24.

Josephine knot

This is an ornamental ring, consisting of the first half of a double stitch worked a specified number of times.

For left-handed pupils

The directions for each stitch apply to both the right and left-handed. The left-handed work from right to left. Place a pocket mirror to the left of each illustration and the exact working position will be reflected.

Abbreviations
Tatting   r(s) – ring(s); sr – small ring; lr – large ring; ds – double stitch; p – picot; smp – small picot; lp – long picot; sep – separated; cl – close; rw – reverse work; sp – space; ch(s) – chain(s); tog – together.

Tatting tips

Milward tatting shuttle is light and easy to use. It has been shaped so that it lies easily between the fingers and will not slip out of position while in use. It has been designed to produce an evenly controlled tension and is capable of carrying a good supply of Mercer-Crochet.

Beginners should always use a coarse Mercer-Crochet Cotton. This shows the formation of each stitch and helps to demonstrate clearly the way in which the varying sequences of stitches build up the patterns.

Start by learning the Double Stitch. This is the basis of all tatting designs.

To join threads
(a)   When ball and shuttle threads are used, a knot can be avoided at the beginning of the work by filling the shuttle and commencing the ring without cutting the thread.
(b)   Make a flat knot, eg a Reef Knot or a Weaver's Knot close to the base of the last ring or chain. Do not cut off the ends as the strain during working may loosen the knot.

To finish off ends
Make a flat knot, eg a Reef Knot or a Weaver's Knot close to the base of the last ring or chain. Do not cut off the ends as the strain during working may loosen the knot. With a single strand of Mercer-Crochet Cotton, oversew the ends neatly to the wrong side of the work (see diagram).

Winding the shuttle
Wind the thread round the centre of the shuttle. Do not wind the thread beyond the edge of the shuttle. When making motifs it is advisable to count the number of turns of thread round the shuttle so that the amount of thread used to make one motif can be assessed. This will prevent unnecessary joining of thread.

Coats Chain Mercer-Crochet Cotton No.20 (20 g).
2 balls. This model is worked in shade 402 (Lt Rose Pink), but any other shade of Mercer-Crochet may be used.
Milward tatting shuttle.
50 cm heavy green fabric, 122 cm (approximately 48 in.) wide.
NB The above quantity is sufficient for 1 Centre-piece and 2 Place Mats.

Tension
Depth of Strip – 4 cm (1½ in.) approximately.

Measurements
Centrepiece – 34.5 × 40.5 cm (13½ × 16 in.).
Place Mat – 28 × 35.5 cm (11 × 14 in.).

Centrepiece
Double trimming (First strip)
Tie ball and shuttle threads together. R of 2 ds, 6 ps
sep by 1 ds, 2 ds, cl, rw. * Ch of 12 ds, 2 ps sep by
12 ds, 3 ds. R of 2 ds, 6 ps sep by 1 ds, 2 ds, cl, rw.
Ch of 3 ds, 4 ps sep by 1 ds, join to second last p on
second last r, 1 ds, 4 ps sep by 1 ds, 3 ds, rw. (R of
2 ds, p, 1 ds, join to second last p on previous r, 1 ds,
4 ps sep by 1 ds, 2 ds, cl, rw. Ch of 3 ds, 9 ps sep by
1 ds, 3 ds, rw) 5 times. R of 2 ds, p, 1 ds, join to second
last p on previous r, 1 ds, 4 ps sep by 1 ds, 2 ds, cl.
* Ch of 3 ds, join to corresponding p on adjacent ch,
12 ds, p, 12 ds, rw. R of 2 ds, p, 1 ds, join to centre p
on adjacent ch, 1 ds, 4 ps sep by 1 ds, 2 ds, cl, rw.
Ch of 12 ds, 2 ps sep by 12 ds, 3 ds. R of 2 ds, 6 ps sep
by 1 ds, 2 ds, cl, rw. Ch of 3 ds, 4 ps sep by 1 ds, 1 ds,
join to second last p on second last r, 1 ds, 4 ps sep
by 1 ds, 3 ds, rw. R of 2 ds, p, 1 ds, join to second last
p on previous r, 1 ds, 4 ps sep by 1 ds, 2 ds, cl, rw.
Ch of 3 ds, 4 ps sep by 1 ds, 1 ds, join to corresponding
p on adjacent ch, 1 ds, 4 ps sep by 1 ds, 3 ds, rw. (R of
2 ds, p, 1 ds, join to second last p on previous r, 1 ds,
4 ps sep by 1 ds, 2 ds, cl, rw. Ch of 3 ds, 9 ps sep by
1 ds, 3 ds, rw) 4 times. R of 2 ds, p, 1 ds, join to second
last p on previous r, 1 ds, 4 ps sep by 1 ds, 2 ds, cl;
repeat from * 8 times more. Ch of 3 ds, join to corresponding p on adjacent ch, 12 ds, p, 12 ds, rw. R of
2 ds, p, 1 ds, join to centre p on adjacent ch, 1 ds,
4 ps sep by 1 ds, 2 ds, cl. Tie ends, cut and oversew
neatly on wrong side.

Second strip
Tie ball and shuttle threads together. R of 2 ds, 6 ps
sep by 1 ds, 2 ds, cl, rw. * Ch of 12 ds, join to first free

p on large ch of First Strip, 12 ds, p, 3 ds. R of 2 ds,
6 ps sep by 1 ds, 2 ds, cl, rw. Ch of 3 ds, 4 ps sep by
1 ds, join to second last p on second last r, 1 ds, 4 ps
sep by 1 ds, 3 ds, rw. (R of 2 ds, p, 1 ds, join to second
last p on previous r, 1 ds, 4 ps sep by 1 ds, 2 ds, cl,
rw. Ch of 3 ds, 9 ps sep by 1 ds, 3 ds, rw) 5 times. R of
2 ds, p, 1 ds, join to second last p on previous r, 1 ds,
4 ps sep by 1 ds, 2 ds, cl. Ch of 3 ds, join to corresponding p on adjacent ch, 12 ds, join to next free p on
First Strip, 12 ds, rw. R of 2 ds, p, 1 ds, join to adjacent
ch, 1 ds, 4 ps sep by 1 ds, 2 ds, cl, rw and complete to
correspond with first strip joining to free p of each
large ch as before.

Make one more Double Trimming.

Place mat (make 2)
Double trimming   Work as Double Trimming for
Centrepiece, working repeat 6 times more instead of 8.
Single trimming   Work as first strip of Double Trim-
ming for Centrepiece.

Damp and pin out to measurements.

To make up
Cut 1 piece of fabric 38 × 44.5 cm (15 × 17½ in.) for
centrepiece and 2 pieces 32 × 39.5 cm (12½ × 15½ in.)
for place mats.

Turn back 1.5 cm (½ in.) hems, mitre corners and
slipstitch in position. Sew one double trimming to
each end of centrepiece. Sew one double trimming to
one end and one single trimming to other end of each
place mat. (See illustration.)

Tatted Cushion

Coats Chain Mercer-Crochet Cotton No.20 (20 g).
3 balls. This model is worked in shade 943 (Viridian), but any other shade of Mercer-Crochet may be used.
Milward tatting shuttle.
70 cm fine/medium gold fabric, 90 cm (approximately 36 in.) wide.

Tension
Depth of Strip – 5 cm (2 in.).
Length of Strip – 30.5 cm (12 in.).

Measurements
30.5 × 46 cm (12 × 18 in.).

First strip

1st Row: Tie ball and shuttle threads together. R of 5 ds, p, 3 ds, p, 2 ds, cl, rw. Ch of 3 ds, rw. (R of 2 ds, join to last p of previous r, 5 ds, 2 ps sep by 5 ds, 2 ds, cl, rw. Ch of 3 ds, rw) 7 times. R of 2 ds, join to last p of previous r, 3 ds, p, 5 ds, cl, rw. * Ch of 3 ds, 3 ps sep by 3 ds, 3 ds, rw. R of 5 ds, join to last p of previous r, 5 ds, cl. R of 5 ds, p, 5 ds, cl, rw. Ch of 3 ds, 3 ps sep by 3 ds, 3 ds, rw. R of 5 ds, join to p of previous r, 3 ds, p, 2 ds, cl, rw. ** Ch of 2 ds, rw. (R of 2 ds, join to last p of previous r, 5 ds, 2 ps sep by 5 ds, 2 ds, cl, rw. Ch of 2 ds, rw) twice. R of 2 ds, join to last p of previous r, 3 ds, p, 5 ds, cl, rw; repeat from * 7 times more ending last repeat at **. Ch of 3 ds, rw. (R of 2 ds, join to last p of previous r, 5 ds, 2 ps sep by 5 ds, 2 ds, cl, rw. Ch of 3 ds, rw) 7 times. R of 2 ds, join to last p of previous r, 3 ds, p, 5 ds, cl, rw. Ch of 3 ds, p, 3 ds, join to corresponding p on adjacent ch, 3 ds, p, 3 ds, rw. *** R of 5 ds, join to last p of previous r, 5 ds, cl. R of 5 ds, p, 5 ds, cl, rw. Ch of 3 ds, p, 3 ds, join to corresponding p on next ch, 3 ds, p, 3 ds, rw. R of 5 ds, join to p of previous r, 3 ds, p, 2 ds, cl, rw. Ch of 2 ds, rw. (R of 2 ds, join to last p of previous r, 5 ds, 2 ps sep by 5 ds, 2 ds, cl, rw. Ch of 2 ds, rw) twice. R of 2 ds, join to last p of previous r, 3 ds, p, 5 ds, cl, rw. Ch of 3 ds, p, 3 ds, join to corresponding p on next ch, 3 ds, p, 3 ds, rw; repeat from *** 6 times more. R of 5 ds, join to last p of previous r, 5 ds, cl. R of 5 ds, join to p of first r, 5 ds, cl, rw. Ch of 3 ds, p, 3 ds, join to corresponding p on next ch, 3 ds, p, 3 ds, join to base of first r. Tie ends, cut and oversew neatly on wrong side.

2nd Row: Tie ball and shuttle threads together. Attach thread to joining p of first and last rs on previous row. ** Ch of 5 ds, join by shuttle thread to next free p, (smp, 9 ds, join by shuttle thread to next free p) 6 times, smp, 5 ds, join by shuttle thread to next joining p, rw. Ch of 7 ds, join by shuttle thread to next smp, (smp, 11 ds, join by shuttle thread to next smp) 6 times, smp, 7 ds, miss 5 ds, join by shuttle thread to next joining p, rw. Ch of 3 ds, 3 ps sep by 2 ds, 3 ds, join by shuttle thread to next smp, (3 ds, 6 ps sep by 2 ds, 3 ds, join by shuttle thread to next smp) 6 times, 3 ds, 3 ps sep by 2 ds, 3 ds, join by shuttle thread to same joining p as previous chs. * Ch of 2 ds, 3 ps sep by 2 ds, 2 ds, join by shuttle thread to next joining p. Ch of 5 ds, join by shuttle thread to next p, smp, 7 ds, join by shuttle thread to next p, smp, 5 ds, join by shuttle thread to next joining p, rw. Ch of 7 ds, join by shuttle thread to next smp, smp, 9 ds, join by shuttle thread to next smp, smp, 7 ds, working over previous chs join by shuttle thread to next joining p, rw. Ch of 3 ds, 3 ps sep by 2 ds, 3 ds, join by shuttle thread to next smp, 3 ds, 5 ps sep by 2 ds, 3 ds, join by shuttle thread to next smp, 3 ds, 3 ps sep by 2 ds, 3 ds,

join by shuttle thread to same joining p as previous chs; repeat from * 6 times more. Ch of 2 ds, 3 ps sep by 2 ds, join by shuttle thread to next joining p; repeat from ** once more. Tie ends, cut and oversew neatly on wrong side.

Second strip

1st Row: As 1st row of First Strip.

2nd Row: Tie ball and shuttle threads together. Attach thread to joining p of first and last rs on previous row. Ch of 5 ds, join by shuttle thread to next free p, (smp, 9 ds, join by shuttle thread to next free p) 6 times, smp, 5 ds, join by shuttle thread to next joining p, rw. Ch of 7 ds, join by shuttle thread to next smp, (smp, 11 ds, join by shuttle thread to next smp) 6 times, smp, 7 ds, join by shuttle thread to same joining p as previous ch, rw. Ch of 3 ds, 3 ps sep by 2 ds, 3 ds, join by shuttle thread to next smp, (3 ds, 6 ps sep by 2 ds, 3 ds, join by shuttle thread to next smp) 5 times, 3 ds, 2 ps sep by 2 ds, 2 ds, join to corresponding p on first strip, 2 ds, join to next p on first strip, 2 ds, 2 ps sep by 2 ds, 3 ds, join by shuttle thread to next smp on second strip, 3 ds, 3 ps sep by 2 ds, 3 ds, join by shuttle thread to same joining p as previous chs. * Ch of 2 ds, 3 ps sep by 2 ds, 2 ds, join by shuttle thread to next joining p. Ch of 5 ds, join by shuttle thread to next p, smp, 7 ds, join by shuttle thread to next p, smp, 5 ds, join by shuttle thread to next joining p, rw. Ch of 7 ds, join by shuttle thread to next smp, smp, 9 ds, join by shuttle thread to next smp, smp, 7 ds, working over previous chs join by shuttle thread to next joining p, rw. Ch of 3 ds, 3 ps sep by 2 ds, 3 ds, join by shuttle thread to next smp, 3 ds, p, 2 ds, join to corresponding p on first strip, (2 ds, join to next p on first strip) twice, 2 ds, p, 3 ds, join to next smp on second strip, 3 ds, 3 ps sep by 2 ds, 3 ds, join by shuttle thread to same joining p as previous chs; repeat from * 6 times more. Ch of 2 ds, 3 ps sep by 2 ds, 2 ds, join to next joining p. Ch of 5 ds, join by shuttle thread to next free p, (smp, 9 ds, join by shuttle thread to next free p) 6 times, smp, 5 ds, join by shuttle thread to next joining p, rw. Ch of 7 ds, join by shuttle thread to next smp, (smp, 11 ds, join by shuttle thread to next smp) 6 times, smp, 7 ds, join by shuttle thread to same joining p as previous ch, rw. Ch of 3 ds, 3 ps sep by 2 ds, 3 ds, join by shuttle thread to next smp, 3 ds, 2 ps sep by 2 ds, 2 ds, join to corresponding p on first strip, 2 ds, join to next p on first strip, 2 ds, 2 ps sep by 2 ds, 3 ds, join by shuttle thread to next smp on second strip, (3 ds, 6 ps sep by 2 ds, 3 ds, join by shuttle thread to next smp) 5 times, 3 ds, 3 ps sep by 2 ds, 3 ds, join to next joining p. Ch of 2 ds, 3 ps sep by 2 ds, 2 ds, join by shuttle thread to next joining p and complete as first strip. Tie ends, cut and oversew neatly on wrong side.

Work 7 more strips, joining each as second strip was joined to first.

Damp and pin out to measurements.

To make up
Cut 2 pieces of fabric 50.5 × 35.5 cm (20 × 14 in.).

Place tatting centrally to first piece of fabric and sew neatly in position. Place second piece of fabric to first piece, right sides together and machine stitch 1.5 cm ($\frac{1}{2}$ in.) from edge, leaving an opening to insert pad. Trim seams, neaten corners and turn to right side. Insert pad and sew opening.

Motif Tray Cloth

Coats Chain Mercer-Crochet Cotton No.20 (20 g).
4 balls. This model is worked in shade 510 (Cobalt
Blue), but any other shade of Mercer-Crochet may be
used.
   Milward tatting shuttle.

Tension
Size of Motif – 4.5 cm (1¾ in.).

Measurements
35.5 × 53.5 cm (14 × 21 in.).

First motif
1st Row: R of 3 ds, (lp, 4 ds, smp, 4 ds) 3 times, lp,
4 ds, smp, 1 ds, cl, rw. Tie ends, cut and oversew
neatly on wrong side.
2nd Row: Tie ball and shuttle threads together. R of
3 ds, p, 3 ds, join to any lp on previous row, 3 ds, p,
3 ds, cl, rw. * Ch of p, 12 ds, join by shuttle thread to
next smp on previous row, p, 12 ds, rw. R of 3 ds, p,
3 ds, join to next lp on previous row, 3 ds, p, 3 ds, cl,
rw; repeat from * 3 times more omitting r at end of last
repeat, joining last ch to same place as join. Tie ends,
cut and oversew neatly on wrong side.
3rd Row: Tie ball and shuttle threads together.
Attach thread to first p on previous row. * Ch of p,
13 ds, join by shuttle thread to next p on previous
row; repeat from * joining last ch to same place as
join. Tie ends, cut and oversew neatly on wrong side.
4th Row: Tie ball and shuttle threads together. Attach
thread to first p on previous row. * Ch of p, 4 ds, 5 ps
sep by 2 ds, 4 ds, join to next p on previous row;
repeat from * joining last ch to same place as join. Tie
ends, cut and oversew neatly on wrong side.

Second motif
Work as first motif for 3 rows.
4th Row: Tie ball and shuttle threads together. Attach
thread to first p on previous row. (Ch of p, 4 ds, 2 ps
sep by 2 ds, 2 ds, join to corresponding p on first
motif, 2 ds, 2 ps sep by 2 ds, 4 ds, join by shuttle
thread to next p on second motif) twice. Complete as
first motif.
   Make 8 rows of 12 motifs, joining adjacent sides as
second motif was joined to first motif.
   Damp and pin out to measurements.

KNITTING

Whether your home is modern, contemporary or traditional in its furnishing, or perhaps a mixture of all three, you will find in this selection an exquisite addition to decorate your home.

Abbreviations

KNITTING

K – knit; P – purl; st(s) – stitch(es); beg – begin(ning); patt – pattern; sl – slip; psso – pass slip stitch(es) over; tog – together; tbl – through back of loop(s); yfd – yarn forward; yrn – yarn round needle; m2 – make 2 by working K1 P1 and K1 into next st; butterfly – cast on 3 sts, drop next 3 sts thus forming a 'ladder', insert right hand needle under the 6 strands and K one st, yfd, then insert right hand needle under the 6 strands again and K one st, cast on 3 sts.

Knitting tips

Thread

Coats Chain Mercer-Crochet Cotton is the ideal medium for working knitted lace as it is fine and has a mercerized finish which allows the design to retain its clarity and traditional delicacy. Bear in mind however that cotton is less elastic than wool, and in order to produce a satisfactory texture, fine needles, as quoted must be used. Remember to keep the working thread fairly tight and the tension even and regular. When changing from knitting with wool or synthetics to knitting with cotton it is advisable to work a practice piece first to establish the change-over.

Needles

Milward Disc knitting needles are recommended. In some cases needles with points at both ends are required and in other cases a circular knitting needle is essential depending upon the number of stitches to be coped with in the chosen design. Where two needles are quoted, use the ordinary knitting pins with knob ends, to prevent the stitches from slipping off. The appropriate needles will, of course, be quoted in the working instructions for each individual design.

Crochet hooks

In modern lace knitting, crocheting-off was adopted as a new method to give the lace pieces a more dainty finish. This does not require an expert knowledge of crochet, as only the working of chain and double crochet is needed to follow the instructions.

Stitches

The knitting stitches used for the working of this craft are very few and simple to do.

How to Knit

1 Casting On

With 2 needles

(a) Begin with a slip knot and put the needles into it as shown.

   * Pass the thread from the ball round and between the points of the needles.

(d) This shows how to arrange the cast-on stitches for working in rounds.

(b) With the right hand needle pull through a loop.

Thumb method

(e) Leave an end of the thread and make a slip knot. Put the needle into it. Pass the end over the thumb as shown and knit into the loop thus made. Draw out the thumb and repeat for the number of stitches required.

(c) Put this loop on to the left hand needle, slip right hand needle to back of left hand needle and continue from * in this way for the number of stitches required.

2 Knit Stitch

The four stages of working a knot or plain stitch.

(a)   Put the right hand needle into the loop under the left hand needle as shown.

(b)   Pass the thread round and between the points of the needles.

(c)   Pull a loop through on the point of the right hand needle. This makes the new stitch. Now slip the old stitch from the left hand needle.

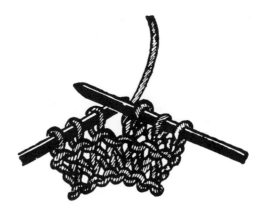

(d)   The new stitch is complete and the right hand needle is ready to be put into the next stitch.

3   Purl Stitch

Put the right hand needle through the loop as shown. Pass the thread round the point of the needle and pull a loop through. Slip old stitch from left hand needle.

4   Decreasing

The two most usual methods of decreasing.

(a)   Knit two together.
Put the right hand needle through two loops and knit in the ordinary way.

(b)   Pass slip stitch over
Put the right hand needle into the loop on left hand needle and slip stitch off. Knit next stitch. Put the point of the left hand needle into the slipped stitch and lift it over the knitted stitch.

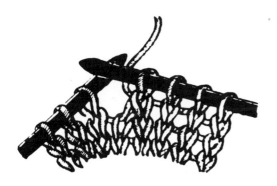

(c)   Movement completed.

5   Increasing

The four most usual ways of increasing.

(a)   *Knit twice into stitch*

Knit into the stitch in the ordinary way and before dropping the loop off the needle, knit into the back of it and slip off needle.

(b)   *Pick up thread between stitches*
This shows the thread which has to be picked up, put back on the left hand needle ready for knitting.

(c)   *Knitting into stitch from row below*
The loop picked up ready for putting on the left hand needle for knitting.

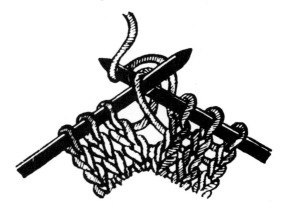

(d)   *Pick up thread between stitches and knit into back of loop*
The loop has been picked up and put on left hand needle. The right hand needle is put through the back of the stitch which twists it and prevents a hole being made.

6 Matching Increasing and Decreasing

(a) The method of knitting twice into a stitch produces the effect of a horizontal bar in the knitting which automatically matches as shown here.

(b) To produce a matched effect when decreasing it is necessary to work 'slip one, knit one, pass the slipped stitch over' on the right and 'knit two together' on the left.

7 'Making' Stitches for Lace Patterns

(a) *Thread forward*
Bring the thread to the front of the work and knit the next stitch in the ordinary way.

(b) *Thread round needle*
This is the same method as 7(a) when worked between purl stitches.

(c) *Thread over needle*
The same method when worked between a knit and a purl stitch.

8 Casting Off

(a) *Simple casting off*
Knit the first two stitches, then with the left hand needle, lift the first loop over the second. Continue knitting a stitch and lifting the loop of the previous stitch over.

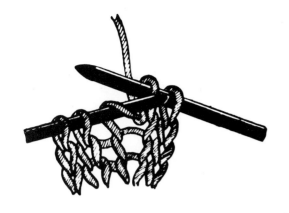

(b) *Double casting off*

When an extra elastic edge is needed, cast off twice in each stitch as shown. The stitch is knitted but the loop is left on the needle. The previous loop is then passed over the next one and the loop left on the needle is knitted. The previous loop is then passed over it in the ordinary way.

(c) *Crochet casting off*

For fine work some people use this method of finishing. As shown, each loop is hooked through the last.

Curtain (see plate 15 page 39)

Coats Chain Mercer-Crochet Cotton No.10 (20 g). 6 balls. This model is worked in White, but any shade of Mercer-Crochet may be used.
    Two 2.50 (no.12) Milward Disc knitting needles.
    Milward steel crochet hook 1.50 (no.2½).

Tension
2 patterns – 8 cm ($3\frac{1}{4}$ in.) in width.

Measurements
Width – 91.5 cm (36 in.).
Depth – 48 cm (19 in.) excluding loops.
    Note: This curtain can be made to any size by casting on a multiple of 12 sts plus 4 and working for length required.
    Cast on 268 sts and P 1 row.

Begin pattern
1st Row (right side): K2 tog, yrn twice, sl 1, K1, psso, * K8, K2 tog, yrn twice, sl 1, K1, psso; repeat from * to end.
2nd Row: P, working P1 and K1 into each 'yrn twice' of previous row.
3rd Row: K2 tog, yrn twice, sl 1, K1, psso, * K2, K2 tog, yrn 3 times, sl 1, K1, psso, K2, K2 tog, yrn twice, sl 1, K1, psso; repeat from * to end.
4th Row: P1, work P1 and K1 into 'yrn twice', * P4, work P1 into 'yrn 3 times' dropping extra loops, P4, work P1 and K1 into 'yrn twice'; repeat from * to last st, P1.
5th Row: K2 tog, yrn twice, sl 1, K1, psso, * K1, K2 tog, yfd, K1, yfd, sl 1, K1, psso, K1, K2 tog, yrn twice, sl 1, K1, psso; repeat from * to end.
6th Row: As 2nd row.
7th Row: K2 tog, yrn twice, sl 1, K1, psso, * K2 tog, K3, sl 1, K1, psso, K2 tog, yrn twice, sl 1, K1, psso; repeat from * to end.
8th Row: As 2nd row.
9th Row: K2 tog, yrn twice, * sl 1, K2 tog, psso, butterfly, sl 1, K2 tog, psso, yrn twice; repeat from * to last 2 sts, sl 1, K1, psso.
10th Row: P1, work P1 and K1 into 'yrn twice', * P4, P2 tog, P5, work P1 and K1 into 'yrn twice'; repeat from * to last st, P1.
    These 10 rows form the patt.
    Repeat the patt 19 times then work 1st and 2nd rows again. Cast off.

Edging
1st Row: With right side facing attach thread to right hand corner of top edge, 3 dc into same place at corner, work a row across top edge having a multiple

of 11 dc, 3 dc into same place at next corner, continue to work a row of dc round three remaining sides having a multiple of 2 dc across each side and 3 dc into same place as corners, ending with 1 ss into first dc.

2nd Row: 1 dc into same place as ss, 3 dc into next (corner) dc, 1 dc into each dc working 3 dc into centre dc at each corner, 1 ss into first dc.

3rd Row: 1 dc into same place as ss, * 1 ss into front loop of each of next 4 dc, 22 ch, 1 ss into back loop of same dc, 1 ss into each of 22 ch, *** 1 ss into front loop of each of next 6 dc, 22 ch, 1 ss into back loop of same dc, 1 ss into each of 22 ch, 1 ss into back loop of next dc; repeat from * along top edge ending last repeat at ***, 1 ss into front loop of each of next 4 dc, ** 1 dc into next dc, 3 ch, 1 ss into last dc – a picot made, 1 dc into next dc; repeat from ** to within 3 dc at next corner, 1 dc into next dc, into next dc work 1 dc a picot and 1 dc, 1 dc into next dc; repeat from first ** twice more omitting 1 dc and corner at end of last repeat, 1 ss into first dc. Fasten off.

Damp and pin out to measurements.

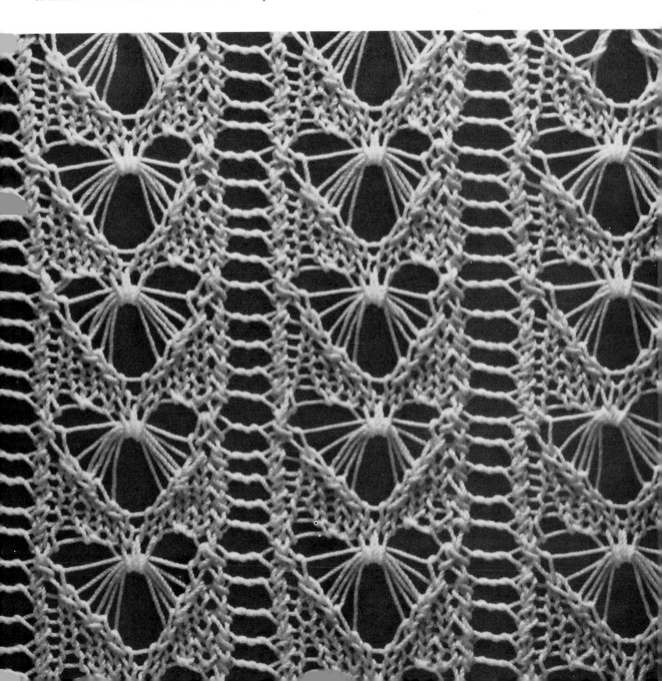

Dinner Set (see plate 16 page 40)

Coats Chain Mercer-Crochet Cotton No.20 (20 g).
2 balls. This model is worked in shade 621 (Lt French Blue), but any other shade of Mercer-Crochet may be used.
Set of four 2.50 (no.12) Milward Disc knitting needles with points at both ends.
Milward steel crochet hook 1.00 (no.4).
The above quantity is sufficient for two place mats and two glass mats.

Tension
8 sts and 11 rows to 2.5 cm (1 in.) square over stocking stitch.

Measurements
Place mat – 33 cm (13 in.) in diameter.
Glass mat – 18 cm (7 in.) in diameter.

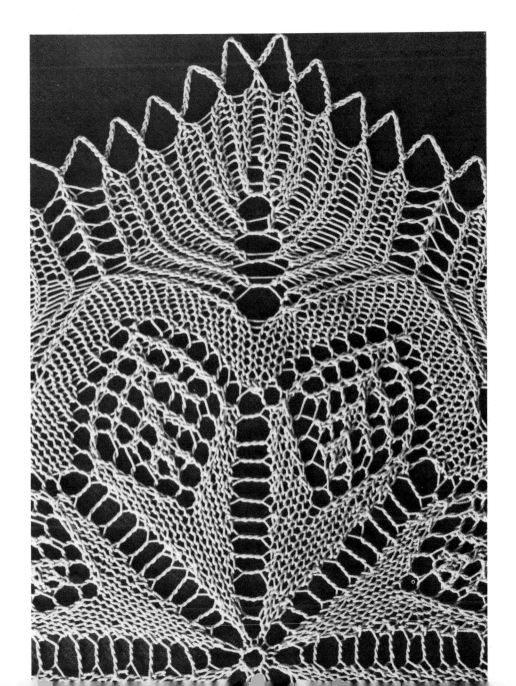

Place mat

Cast on 8 sts, 3 sts on each of 2 needles and 2 sts on 3rd needle. K 1 round.

1st Round: * K1, yrn twice; repeat from * to end. 24 sts.

2nd and **alternate Rounds** unless otherwise stated: K, working K1 and P1 into each 'yrn twice' of previous round.

3rd Round: * K2, yrn twice, K1; repeat from * to end. 40 sts.

5th Round: * K1, K2 tog, yrn twice, sl 1, K1, psso; repeat from * to end.

7th Round: * K3, yrn twice, K2; repeat from * to end. 56 sts.

9th Round: * K2, K2 tog, yrn twice, sl 1, K1, psso, K1; repeat from * to end.

11th Round: * K4, yrn twice, K3; repeat from * to end. 72 sts.

13th Round: * K3, K2 tog, yrn twice, sl 1, K1, psso, K2; repeat from * to end.

15th Round: * K5, yrn twice, K4; repeat from * to end. 88 sts.

17th Round: Before commencing round K first st from left-hand needle on to right-hand needle, * yfd, K3, K2 tog, yrn twice, sl 1, K1, psso, K2, K2 tog; repeat from * to end.

19th Round: * Yfd, K1 tbl, yfd, sl 1, K1, psso, K3, yrn twice, K3, K2 tog; repeat from * to end. 104 sts.

21st Round: * (Yfd, K1) 3 times, yfd, sl 1, K1, psso, K1, K2 tog, yrn twice, sl 1, K1, psso, K1, K2 tog; repeat from * to end. 120 sts.

23rd Round: * Yfd, K1, yfd, sl 1, K1, psso, K1, K2 tog, yfd, K1, yfd, sl 1, K1, psso, K2, yrn twice, K2, K2 tog; repeat from * to end. 136 sts.

25th Round: * Yfd, K1, yfd, sl 1, K1, psso, yfd, sl 1, K2 tog, psso, yfd, K2 tog, yfd, K1, yfd, sl 1, K2 tog, psso, yfd, K2, yfd, sl 1, K2 tog, psso; repeat from * to end.

26th and **alternate Rounds:** K.

27th Round: Before commencing round K first st on left-hand needle on to right-hand needle, * sl 1, K1, psso, yfd, sl 1, K1, psso, K1, (K2 tog, yfd) 3 times, K4, yfd, sl 1, K1, psso, yfd; repeat from * to end.

29th Round: * Sl 1, K1, psso, yfd, sl 1, K2 tog, psso, (yfd, K2 tog) twice, yfd, K6, yfd, sl 1, K1, psso, yfd; repeat from * to end.

31st Round: * Sl 1, K1, psso, K1, (K2 tog, yfd) twice, K8, yfd, sl 1, K1, psso, yfd; repeat from * to end.

33rd Round: * Sl 1, K2 tog, psso, yfd, K2 tog, yfd, K10, yfd, sl 1, K1, psso, yfd; repeat from * to end.

35th Round: * K1, K2 tog, yfd, K4, K2 tog, yrn twice, sl 1, K1, psso, K4, yfd, sl 1, K1, psso; repeat from * to end.

36th and **alternate Rounds:** As 2nd round.

37th Round: Before commencing round K first 2 sts on left-hand needle on to right-hand needle, * yfd, K4, K2 tog, (m2) twice, sl 1, K1, psso, K4, yfd, sl 1, K2 tog, psso; repeat from * to end. 152 sts.

39th Round: * K4, K2 tog, K1 tbl, P1, K1 tbl, yrn twice, K1 tbl, P1, K1 tbl, sl 1, K1, psso, K3, K2 tog, yfd; repeat from * to end.

40th and **alternate Rounds:** As 2nd round working K tbl and P into tbl and P sts of previous round.

41st Round: * K3, K2 tog, K1 tbl, P1, K1 tbl, (m2) twice, K1 tbl, P1, K1 tbl, sl 1, K1, psso, K4; repeat from * to end. 168 sts.

43rd Round: * K2, K2 tog, (K1 tbl, P1, K1 tbl) twice, yrn twice, (K1 tbl, P1, K1 tbl) twice, sl 1, K1 psso, K3; repeat from * to end.

45th Round: * K1, K2 tog, (K1 tbl, P1, K1 tbl) twice, (m2) twice, (K1 tbl, P1, K1 tbl) twice, sl 1, K1, psso, K2; repeat from * to end. 184 sts.

47th Round: * K2 tog, (K1 tbl, P1, K1 tbl) 3 times, yrn twice, (K1 tbl, P1, K1 tbl) 3 times, sl 1, K1, psso, K1; repeat from * to end.

49th Round: Before commencing round K first st on left-hand needle on to right-hand needle, * (K1 tbl, P1, K1 tbl) 3 times, (m2) twice, (K1 tbl, P1, K1 tbl) 3 times, sl 1, K2 tog, psso; repeat from * to end. 200 sts.

51st Round: * (K1 tbl, P1, K1 tbl) 4 times, yfd, (K1 tbl, P1, K1 tbl) 4 times, yfd, K1 tbl, yfd; repeat from * to end. 224 sts.

53rd Round: * (K1 tbl, P1, K1 tbl) 4 times, m2, (K1 tbl, P1, K1 tbl) 4 times, yfd, sl 1, K2 tog, psso, yfd; repeat from * to end. 240 sts.

55th, 57th and **59th Rounds:** * (K1 tbl, P1, K1 tbl) 9 times, yfd, sl 1, K2 tog, psso, yfd; repeat from * to end.

60th Round: Work sts as set. 240 sts.

Edging
Using crochet hook work * 1 dc into next 3 sts and slip off, 10 ch; repeat from * ending with 1 ss into first dc. Fasten off.

Glass mat

Work as place mat until 34th round has been completed.

Edging
Before commencing crochet K first 3 sts on left-hand needle on to right-hand needle. Using crochet hook work * (1 dc into next 3 sts and slip off, 10 ch) 4 times, 1 dc into next 5 sts and slip off, 10 ch; repeat from * ending with 1 ss into first dc. Fasten off.

Damp and pin out to measurements.

Coffee Table Mat

Coats Chain Mercer-Crochet Cotton No.20 (20 g).
3 balls. This model is worked in shade 787 (Lt Moss Green), but any other shade of Mercer-Crochet may be used.
Five 2.50 (no.12) Milward Disc knitting needles with points at both ends.

One 2.50 (no.12) Milward circular knitting needle 60 cm (24 in.) long.
Milward steel crochet hook 1.00 (no.4).

Tension
8 sts and 11 rows to 2.5 cm (1 in.) square over stocking stitch.

Measurement

51 cm (20 in.) square.

Cast on 8 sts, 2 on each of 4 needles and work 1 round K tbl. Mark beg of round. The instructions and number of sts is given for one side only, repeat for other three sides.

1st Round: K1 tbl, yfd, K twice into next st, yfd. 5 sts.

2nd Round: K1 tbl, K1, K2 tbl, K1.

3rd Round: K1 tbl, yrn twice, (K2 tbl, yrn twice) twice. 11 sts.

4th and following **alternate Rounds:** K, working tbl all sts worked 'tbl' in previous round, and K1 and P1 into each 'yrn twice' where they occur.

5th Round: K1 tbl, yrn twice, K1 tbl, (K2 tog, yrn twice, sl 1, K1, psso) twice, K1 tbl, yrn twice. 15 sts.

7th Round: K1 tbl, yrn twice, K1, (K2 tog, yrn twice, sl 1, K1, psso) 3 times, K1 yrn twice. 19 sts.

9th Round: K1 tbl, yrn twice, K1, (K2 tog, yrn twice, sl 1, K1, psso) 4 times, K1, yrn twice. 23 sts.

11th Round: K1 tbl, yrn twice, K1, (K2 tog, yrn twice, sl 1, K1, psso) 5 times, K1, yrn twice. 27 sts.

13th Round: K1 tbl, yrn twice, K1, (K2 tog, yrn twice, sl 1, K1, psso) 6 times, K1, yrn twice. 31 sts.

15th Round: K1 tbl, yrn twice, K1, (K2 tog, yrn twice, sl 1, K1, psso) 7 times, K1, yrn twice. 35 sts.

17th Round: K1 tbl, yrn twice, K1, (K2 tog, yrn twice, sl 1, K1, psso) 8 times, K1, yrn twice. 39 sts.

19th Round: K1 tbl, yrn twice, K1, (K2 tog, yrn twice, sl 1, K1, psso) 9 times, K1, yrn twice. 43 sts.

21st Round: K1 tbl, yrn twice, K1, (K2 tog, yrn twice, sl 1, K1, psso) twice, K4, (K2 tog, yrn twice, sl 1, K1, psso) 4 times, K4, (K2 tog, yrn twice, sl 1, K1, psso) twice, K1, yrn twice. 47 sts.

23rd Round: K1 tbl, yrn twice, K1, (K2 tog, yrn twice, sl 1, K1, psso) twice, K8, (K2 tog, yrn twice, sl 1, K1, psso) 3 times, K8, (K2 tog, yrn twice, sl 1, K1, psso) twice, K1, yrn twice. 51 sts.

25th Round: K1 tbl, yfd, K3, yrn twice, sl 1, K1, psso, K2 tog, yrn twice, sl 1, K1, psso, K4, K2 tog, yrn twice, sl 1, K1, psso, K4, (K2 tog, yrn twice, sl 1, K1, psso) twice, K4, K2 tog, yrn twice, sl 1, K1, psso, K4, K2 tog, yrn twice, sl 1, K1, psso, K2 tog, yrn twice, sl 1, K1, psso, K3, yfd. 55 sts.

27th Round: K1 tbl, yrn twice, K5, K2 tog, yrn twice, sl 1, K1, psso, K4, (K2 tog, yrn twice, sl 1, K1, psso) twice, K4, K2 tog, yrn twice, sl 1, K1, psso, K4, (K2 tog, yrn twice, sl 1, K1, psso) twice, K4, K2 tog, yrn twice, sl 1, K1, psso, K5, yrn twice. 59 sts.

29th Round: K1 tbl, yrn twice, K1, K2 tog, yrn twice, sl 1, K1, psso, * K8, (K2 tog, yrn twice, sl 1, K1, psso) 3 times **, work from * to ** once more, K8, K2 tog, yrn twice, sl 1, K1, psso, K1, yrn twice. 63 sts.

31st Round: K1 tbl, yrn twice, K1, (K2 tog, yrn twice, sl 1, K1, psso) twice, * K4, (K2 tog, yrn twice, sl 1, K1, psso) 4 times **, work from * to ** once more, K4, (K2 tog, yrn twice, sl 1, K1, psso) twice, K1, yrn twice. 67 sts.

33rd Round: K1 tbl, yrn twice, K1, (K2 tog, yrn twice, sl 1, K1, psso) 16 times, K1, yrn twice. 71 sts.

35th Round: K1 tbl, yrn twice, K1, (K2 tog, yrn twice, sl 1, K1, psso) 3 times, * K4, (K2 tog, yrn twice, sl 1, K1, psso) 4 times **, work from * to ** once more, K4, (K2 tog, yrn twice, sl 1, K1, psso) 3 times, K1, yrn twice. 75 sts.

37th Round: K1 tbl, yfd, K1 tbl, yrn twice, K2 tbl, yrn twice, sl 1, K1, psso, (K2 tog, yrn twice, sl 1, K1, psso) twice, * K4, yfd, K4, (K2 tog, yrn twice, sl 1, K1, psso) 3 times **, work from * to ** once more, K4, yfd, K4, (K2 tog, yrn twice, sl 1, K1, psso) twice, K2 tog, yrn twice, K2 tbl, yrn twice, K1 tbl, yfd. 86 sts.

39th Round: (K1 tbl, yfd) twice, * sl 1, K1, psso, K4, (K2 tog, yrn twice, sl 1, K1, psso) twice, K4, K2 tog, yfd, K1 tbl, yfd **, work from * to ** 3 times more. 88 sts.

41st Round: K1 tbl, * (yfd, K1, K1 tbl, K1, yfd **, sl 1, K1, psso, K3, sl 1, K1, psso, K2 tog, yrn twice, sl 1, K1, psso, K2 tog, K3, K2 tog) 4 times, work from * to ** once more. 82 sts.

43rd Round: K1 tbl, * (yfd, K2 tog, yfd, K1 tbl, yfd, sl 1, K1, psso, yfd **, sl 1, K1, psso, K3, sl 1, K1, psso, K2 tog, K3, K2 tog) 4 times, work from * to ** once more. 76 sts.

45th Round: K1 tbl, * (yfd, K1, K1 tbl, K1, yfd, K1 tbl, yfd, K1, K1 tbl, K1, yfd **, sl 1, K1, psso, K6, K2 tog) 4 times, work from * to ** once more. 88 sts.

Change to circular needle and mark beg of round, also each side if required.

47th Round: K1 tbl, * (yfd, K2 tog, yfd, K1 tbl, yfd, sl 1, K1, psso, yfd, K1 tbl, yfd, K2 tog, yfd, K1 tbl, yfd, sl 1, K1, psso, yfd **, sl 1, K1, psso, K4, K2 tog) 4 times, work from * to ** once more. 100 sts.

49th Round: K1 tbl, * (yfd, K2 tog, K1, yfd, K1 tbl, yfd, K1, sl 1, K1, psso, yfd, K1 tbl, yfd, K2 tog, K1, yfd, K1 tbl, yfd, K1, sl 1, K1, psso, yfd **, sl 1, K1, psso, K2, K2 tog) 4 times, work from * to ** once more. 112 sts.

51st Round: K1 tbl, * (yfd, K2 tog, K2, yfd, K1 tbl, yfd, K2, sl 1, K1, psso, yfd, K1 tbl, yfd, K2 tog, K2, yfd, K1 tbl, yfd, K2, sl 1, K1, psso, yfd **, sl 1, K1, psso, K2 tog) 4 times, work from * to ** once more. 124 sts.

53rd Round: (K1 tbl, yfd) twice, K1, * (K3, yfd, K1 tbl, yfd, K3, sl 1, K1, psso, yfd, K1 tbl, yfd, K2 tog, K3, yfd, K1 tbl, yfd, K3 **, sl 1, K2 tog, psso, K3 tog) 4 times, work from * to ** once more, K1, yfd, K1 tbl, yfd. 132 sts.

55th Round: K1 tbl, yrn twice, K1 tbl, K2 tog, yfd, (sl 1, K1, psso, K7, K2 tog, yfd, K1, K1 tbl, K1, yfd, sl 1, K1, psso, K7, K2 tog) 5 times, yfd, sl 1, K1, psso,

K1 tbl, yrn twice. 126 sts.

57th Round: K1 tbl, yrn twice, K1, K2 tog, yrn twice, sl 1, K1, psso, yfd, (sl 1, K1, psso, K5, K2 tog, yfd, K2 tog, yfd, K1 tbl, yfd, sl 1, K1, psso, yfd, sl 1, K1, psso, K5, K2 tog) 5 times, yfd, K2 tog, yrn twice, sl 1, K1, psso, K1, yrn twice. 122 sts.

59th Round: K1 tbl, yrn twice, K1, K2 tog, yrn twice, sl 1, K1, psso, sl 1, K2 tog, psso, yrn twice, (sl 1, K1, psso, K3, K2 tog, yfd, K2 tog, K1, yfd, K1 tbl, yfd, K1, sl 1, K1, psso, yfd, sl 1, K1, psso, K3, K2 tog, yrn twice) 5 times, sl 1, K2 tog, psso, K2 tog, yrn twice, sl 1, K1, psso, K1, yrn twice. 124 sts.

61st Round: K1 tbl, yrn twice, K1, (K2 tog, yrn twice, sl 1, K1, psso) twice, (K1, yfd, sl 1, K1, psso, K1, K2 tog, yfd, K2 tog, K2, yfd, K1 tbl, yfd, K2, sl 1, K1, psso, yfd, sl 1, K1, psso, K1, K2 tog, yfd, K1) 5 times, (K2 tog, yrn twice, sl 1, K1, psso) twice, K1, yrn twice. 128 sts.

63rd Round: K1 tbl, yrn twice, K1, (K2 tog, yrn twice, sl 1, K1, psso) 3 times, (sl 1, K2 tog, psso, yfd, K2 tog, K3, yfd, K1 tbl, yfd, K3, sl 1, K1, psso, yfd, sl 1, K2 tog, psso, K2 tog, yrn twice, sl 1, K1, psso) 5 times, (K2 tog, yrn twice, sl 1, K1, psso) twice, K1, yrn twice. 122 sts.

65th Round: K1 tbl, yrn twice, K1, (K2 tog, yrn twice, sl 1, K1, psso) 3 times, (K2 tog, yrn twice, sl 1, K1, psso, yfd, sl 1, K1, psso, K7, K2 tog, yfd, K2 tog, yrn twice, sl 1, K1, psso) 5 times, (K2 tog, yrn twice, sl 1, K1, psso) 3 times, K1, yrn twice. 126 sts.

67th Round: K1 tbl, yrn twice, K1, (K2 tog, yrn twice, sl 1, K1, psso) 3 times, K2 tog, yrn twice, (sl 1, K1, psso, K2 tog, yrn twice, K1, yfd, sl 1, K1, psso, K5, K2 tog, yfd, K1, yrn twice, sl 1, K1, psso, K2 tog, yrn twice) 5 times, sl 1, K1, psso, (K2 tog, yrn twice, sl 1, K1, psso) 3 times, K1, yrn twice. 140 sts.

69th Round: K1 tbl, yrn twice, K1, (K2 tog, yrn twice, sl 1, K1, psso) 4 times, (K2 tog, yrn twice, sl 1, K1, psso, K2 tog, yfd, K1, yfd, sl 1, K1, psso, K3, K2 tog, yfd, K1, yfd, sl 1, K1, psso, K2 tog, yrn twice, sl 1, K1, psso) 5 times, (K2 tog, yrn twice, sl 1, K1, psso) 4 times, K1, yrn twice. 144 sts.

71st Round: K twice into next st, yfd, sl 1, K1, psso, K1, (yrn twice, sl 1, K1, psso, K2 tog) 4 times, * yfd, sl 1, K1, psso, K2 tog, yrn twice, sl 1, K1, psso, K2 tog, yfd, sl 1, K1, psso, K1, K2 tog, yfd, sl 1, K1, psso, K2 tog, yrn twice, sl 1, K1, psso, K2 tog **, work from * to ** 4 times more, yfd, (sl 1, K1, psso, K2 tog, yrn twice) 4 times, K1, K2 tog, yfd. 131 sts.

73rd Round: K1 tbl, yrn twice, K1 tbl, * yfd, K1 tbl, yfd, sl 1, K1, psso, K1, (K2 tog, yrn twice, sl 1, K1, psso) 3 times, K1, K2 tog **, (yfd, K1 tbl, yfd, sl 1, K1, psso, K1, K2 tog, yrn twice, sl 1, K1, psso, yfd, sl 1, K2, psso the K2, yfd, K2 tog, yrn twice, sl 1, K1, psso, K1, K2 tog) 5 times, work from * to ** once more, yfd, K1 tbl, yfd. 140 sts.

75th Round: Sl 1, K1, psso, yrn twice, K2 tog, (* yfd, K twice into next st, yfd, K1 tbl, yfd, K twice into next st, yfd **, sl 1, K1, psso, sl 1, K1, psso, K2 tog, yrn twice, sl 1, K1, psso, K2 tog, yrn twice, sl 1, K1, psso, K2 tog twice) 7 times, work from * to ** once more. 160 sts.

77th Round: Sl 1, K1, psso, yrn twice, K2 tog, (* yfd, K2 tog, yfd, K1, yfd, K3, yfd, K1, yfd, sl 1, K1, psso, yfd **, sl 1, K1, psso, sl 1, K1, psso, K2 tog, yrn twice, sl 1, K1, psso, K2 tog twice) 7 times, work from * to ** once more. 164 sts.

79th Round: Sl 1, K1, psso, yrn twice, K2 tog, * (yfd, K2 tog) twice, yfd, K5, (yfd, sl 1, K1, psso) twice, yfd **, (sl 1, K1, psso) twice, K2 tog twice, *** work from * to *** 6 times more, work from * to ** once more. 152 sts.

81st Round: Sl 1, K1, psso, yrn twice, K2 tog, (* yfd, K2 tog, yfd, K2 tog, yfd, K7, yfd, sl 1, K1, psso, yfd, sl 1, K1, psso, yfd **, sl 1, K1, psso, K2 tog) 7 times, work from * to ** once more. 154 sts.

82nd Round: K to end.

Edging

Before commencing crochet K 2 sts from left hand needle on to right hand needle.

1st Round: Using crochet hook work * 1 dc into next 3 sts and slip off, 8 ch, ** (1 dc into next 3 sts and slip off, 8 ch) 5 times, 1 dc into next 4 sts and slip off, 8 ch; repeat from ** 6 times more. (1 dc into next 3 sts and slip off, 8 ch) 6 times; repeat from * 3 times more omitting 8 ch at end of last repeat, 4 ch, 1 trip tr into first dc.

2nd Round: (8 ch, 1 dc into next loop) 5 times, * 8 ch, (insert hook into next loop and draw thread through) twice, thread over and draw through all loops on hook, (8 ch, 1 dc into next loop) 4 times; repeat from * 6 times more, (8 ch, 1 dc into next loop) 7 times; repeat from first * 3 times more omitting (8 ch, 1 dc) 5 times at end of last repeat, working last dc into trip tr. Fasten off.

Damp and pin out to measurement.